Prayer Steps to Serenity

ANDREW MURRAY
& L.G. Parkhurst, M.A.

CompCare®
Publishers
Minneapolis, Minnesota

Library of Congress Cataloging-in Publication Data
Murray, Andrew, 1828-1917.
    Prayer steps to serenity: the Twelve Steps with proven
prayer principles/Andrew Murray and L.G. Parkhurst, Jr.
    p. cm.
ISBN: 0-89638-293-1
1. Twelve-step programs—Religious aspects—
Christianity—Meditations. 2. Compulsive behavior—
Patients—Prayer books and devotions—English.
3. Recovering addicts—Prayer books and devotions—
English. I Parkhurst, Louis Gifford, 1946-   . II. Title
BV4596.T88M87 1993   92-39633
248.8'6—dc20   CIP

All biblical quotations are from the New International
Version, copyright 1973, 1978, 1984 by the International
Bible Society.

Cover design by Chris Garborg

Inquiries, orders, and catalog requests should be addressed
to:
CompCare Publishers
3850 Annapolis Lane, Suite 100
Minneapolis, Minnesota 55447
Call toll free 800/328-3330 or 612/559-4800

6   5   4   3   2   1
98   97   96   95   94   93

The Eleventh Step

Sought through prayer and meditation to improve our *conscious contact with God* as we understood Him, praying only for knowledge of His will for us and for the power to carry it out.

The Twelve Steps of Alcoholics Anonymous

Step One
We admitted we were powerless over alcohol—that our lives had become unmanageable.

Step Two
Came to believe that a Power greater than ourselves could restore us to sanity.

Step Three
Made a decision to turn our will and our lives over to the care of God, as we understood Him.

Step Four
Made a searching and fearless moral inventory of our-selves.

Step Five
Admitted to God, to ourselves, and to another human being the exact nature of our wrongs.

Step Six
Were entirely ready to have God remove all these defects of character.

Step Seven
Humbly asked Him to remove our shortcomings.

Step Eight
Made a list of all persons we had harmed, and became willing to make amends to them all.

Step Nine

Made direct amends to such people wherever possible, except when to do so would injure them or others.

Step Ten

Continued to take personal inventory and when we were wrong, promptly admitted it.

Step Eleven

Sought through prayer and meditation to improve our conscious contact with God, as we understood Him, praying only for knowledge of His will for us and the power to carry that out.

Step Twelve

Having had a spiritual awakening as the result of these Steps, we tried to carry this message to alcoholics, and to practice these principles in all our affairs.

The Twelve Steps Adapted for This Book

Step One
We admitted we were powerless over our dependencies—that our lives had become unmanageable.

Step Two
Came to believe that a Power greater than ourselves could restore us to sanity.

Step Three
Made a decision to turn our will and our lives over to the care of God, as we understood Him.

Step Four
Made a searching and fearless moral inventory of ourselves.

Step Five
Admitted to God, to ourselves, and to another human being the exact nature of our wrongs.

Step Six
Were entirely ready to have God remove all these defects of character.

Step Seven
Humbly asked Him to remove our shortcomings.

Step Eight
Made a list of all persons we had harmed, and became willing to make amends to them all.

Step Nine
Made direct amends to such people wherever possible, except when to do so would injure them or others.

Step Ten
Continued to take personal inventory and when we were wrong, promptly admitted it.

Step Eleven
Sought through prayer and meditation to improve our conscious contact with God, as we understood Him, praying only for knowledge of His will for us and the power to carry that out.

Step Twelve
Having had a spiritual awakening as the result of these Steps, we tried to carry this message to others, and to practice these principles in all our affairs.

CONTENTS

THE ELEVENTH STEP 141

THE TWELFTH STEP 155

INTRODUCTION

We are not alone. After working through the Twelve Steps for the first time, either in AA, Al-Anon, or some other recovery group, many of us realize God went before us and with us every step of the way. We now see that a loving, caring God first came and convinced us that we were powerless over the problems, afflictions, compulsions, or dependencies besetting us. God wanted to give us the power we lacked to change. When God came into the midst of our sickness, when His light broke through, we saw clearly that our lives had become unmanageable.

Once convinced of our condition, we turned our lives over to God and received the peace and power of His presence. Then, as we faced our character defects and destructive actions (as painful as this was at the time), we confessed them and found forgiveness. Once forgiven by God, we discovered that other human beings received the grace of God to forgive us as well. What a joy, when wholeness and health returned to us and to our relationships with others!

God has graciously given us a proven Program for recovery. By His grace we can study and follow daily the necessary Steps to overcome and stay close to God. Time-tested principles of prayer that will meet our every need can be a key ingredient to recovery. God wants us to be in conscious contact with Him every day. He waits daily for us to spend time with Him— because He loves us and knows that prayer is our greatest need.

Prayer Steps to Serenity is designed to help anyone work through the Twelve Step Program, no matter where you are in your recovery. Whether you are on your First or Twelfth Step, or preparing to take your Fifth Step, your recovery will be more certain through the daily practice of the prayer principles in this book.

In the early chapters, you may not understand all the teachings in each day's reading. However, if you will record daily your impressions as you follow the readings, you will be able to look back and see the progress you have made with your Twelve Step Program. If you work through this book more than once, your daily record will give you even greater assurance that God is indeed working in your life as He has in the lives of so many others.

You don't have to complete each one of the Twelve Steps during the five allotted readings for each Step. Working through the whole book will give you an overview of what God can do through prayer and the Twelve Steps; this will encourage you to continue working wherever you are in your recovery. Some people with several years of recovery behind them—one day at a time—have needed many months working on each Step before feeling ready for the next one—so don't be discouraged! As you apply these prayer principles to your daily life, your recovery can be achieved more quickly and with greater permanence and stability than if you did not maintain a conscious relationship with God.

You may want to keep a Prayer Step Journal and write your own meditations after you have read the day's reading. The space at the end of each reading can also be used for this as you pray through the Twelve Steps.

I hope you will use this book repeatedly so that you can recognize the progress you are making and give God all the praise and glory for your recovery. You will gain new insights and understanding each time you read through this book. Please feel free to write to me with your suggestions or to share your ideas. I pray this book will be an additional valuable step in your recovery.

With Love in the Risen Lamb,
L. G. Parkhurst, Jr.
P.O. Box 571
Edmond, Oklahoma 73083-0571

The First Step

We admitted we were powerless over our dependencies—that our lives had become unmanageable.

Yet the LORD longs to be gracious to you; he rises to show you compassion. For the LORD is a God of justice. Blessed are all who wait for him!
(Isaiah 30:18)

THE FIRST STEP

We admitted we were powerless over our dependencies—that our lives had become unmanageable.

To take the First Step, I need to admit that I am powerless over my dependencies—perhaps alcohol or some other addiction. And more than this, I need to recognize what my behavior indicates: I am not managing my life very well. Perhaps others have been telling me this over and over again, and I have refused to listen. Perhaps I have been too proud to admit they were right. Perhaps I have not wanted to admit that I could not control every area of my life. In the First Step, I only need to admit these things. When I take the First Step, I go a long way down the road to recovery. As the old Greek proverb says, "Well begun is half done."

When I admit that I am not God, I open the door for God's help. I need to confess that my life is out of control and uncontrollable in certain key areas. I may be able to function okay at work, but I need to face the fact that in many other areas I am hurting myself and others by my behavior.

I need to start down the road of humility to find God and receive God's help. John Bunyan wrote:

> He that is down, needs fear no fall;
> He that is low, no pride.
> He that is humble ever shall
> Have God to be his Guide.

Amazingly, when I humble myself before God, God will not push me further down. God promises to lift up the humble. As St. Augustine wrote of pride and humility, "Pride changed angels into devils; humility makes men into angels." Someone once said of God, "His whole employment is to lift up the humble and to cast down the proud." I thank God for His tireless efforts to make and keep me humble!

As I work through the First Step with prayer, God will quickly lead me to a true estimate of myself—the real meaning of humility—and assure me of His guidance and power to change.

1 | THE SOURCE OF ALL MY POWER

I am the vine, you are the branches. If a man remains in me and I in him, he will bear much fruit; apart from me you can do nothing. (John 15:5)

I can proudly begin to think that I am making myself better and don't need anyone. Yet, apart from God, I am powerless. In fact, apart from God, I am only fighting against God, others, and even myself. Without God, I am unable to make the needed changes in my life.

Jesus offers to change my life when He says, "Apart from me you can do nothing." And in my prayers, I need to also think: *Apart from Him, I can pray nothing.*

Today, I have many reasons to be thankful. For one, Jesus promises that when I come to Him to manage my life, He will unite himself with me. He will dwell within me and never leave me. When I finally admit that my life is out of control and ask Him to give me power to change and be a blessing to others—He will. Through daily prayer, meditation, and obedience, I can open my life to Him and enable Him to live and work in and through me each day. *I may be powerless, but God's power will work in me!*

What a reason for joy and encouragement—the Lord Jesus can work in me! I need to remind myself daily that without God I am powerless. I need to depend on Him to care for me and work through me *every day*, one day at a time—sometimes moment by moment. Whenever I recall *Apart from me you can do nothing*, I need to remember too: *The one who remains in me will bear much fruit.*

PRAYER FOR TODAY

Dear God, help me remember that without you my life is uncontrollable. Too often I fail. Don't let me forget that I am powerless to overcome many things, and apart from you, I can do nothing. So, take control of my life and help me to change.

2 | THE GOOD FIGHT OF FAITH

Fight the good fight of the faith. Take hold of the eternal life to which you were called when you made your good confession in the presence of many witnesses. (1 Timothy 6:12)

When I pray in my own strength, I am disappointed and discouraged. But I have found a struggle that leads to victory. The Scriptures speak of it as "the good fight of the faith." This fight springs from within and I can carry it on by faith. When I get the right understanding of faith, I can stand unmoved in faith.

Jesus is the Author and Finisher of faith. The Bible teaches: "Let us fix our eyes on Jesus, the author and perfecter of our faith, who for the joy set before Him endured the cross, scorning its shame, and sat down at the right hand of the throne of God" (Hebrews 12:2). When I come into a right relationship with Jesus, He assures me of His help and power in prayer each moment of every day.

To receive God's help, I first need to believe in

my heart: *I cannot strive in my own strength and succeed. I need to cast myself at the feet of the Lord Jesus. I will wait on Him in the certain confidence that He will be with me and will work in me.*

Second, I need to commit myself to Him and say, "I will strive in prayer. I will let faith fill my heart. Through faith, I will be strong in the Lord, and in the power of His might."

PRAYER FOR TODAY

This day, dear God, strengthen my faith in you and in your only begotten Son, Jesus. By your Holy Spirit, give me the assurance that I have been adopted into your family. As one of your dear children, reassure me when I doubt and increase my faith. Always be my strength and shield.

3 | THE RIGHT ATTITUDE IN PRAYER

I have fought the good fight, I have finished the race, I have kept the faith. **(2 Timothy 4:7)**

As I pray, if my heart is cold and dark, I cannot force myself into a right attitude. All I can do in these times is bow before God and honestly let Him see my real condition. I need to remind myself that my only hope is in Him. With a childlike trust, I can trust Him to have mercy upon me. I have nothing—He has everything.

I have found that faith in the love of Jesus is the only way I can get into fellowship with God in prayer.

I fight two battles. In the first battle, I try to conquer the spirit of prayerlessness and not rely on my own strength. To win this fight, I give up my restlessness and effort and fall helpless at the feet of my loving Lord Jesus. He will speak the word and my soul will live.

If I have done this, to win the second battle requires deep earnestness and the exercise of all the power God gives me. Through searching prayer, I watch over my heart. I pray for God to reveal to me the least backsliding; I ask Him to help me overcome any proneness I have to fall before temptation.

Above all, to have the right attitude in prayer, I need to surrender to a life of self-sacrifice. God really desires to see this spirit within me. If I surrender to Him, He will work it out for me and give me victory.

Prayer for Today

Dear loving Jesus, help me take all the time I need to wait on you in prayer. I surrender all that I am, all that I have, and all that I hope to be to you. I do not have the power or the faith to win any battles. I want to pray with an attitude that surrenders my will to yours. Cleanse me now and fill me with your Holy Spirit.

4 | GOD MEETS ME IN MY DEFECTS

Now to Him who is able to do immeasurably more than all we ask or imagine, according to His power that is at work within us, to Him be glory . . . forever and ever! (Ephesians 3:20, 21)

How prone I am to backslide, to limit God's power, and to think that God cannot do great things. I have such weak concepts of the promises, power, and personality of God! Too often I have blamed God and others for my failures. When I have been powerless, I have thought God helpless. When my life has been out of control, I have accused God of incompetence. When considering my needs, I have sometimes denounced God for being a poor provider.

I need to ask God to make His character known to me. Each day, I need to admit that I am powerless to overcome my difficulties, and that I need God to help me.

I need to learn that even in my experience God is all-powerful. In daily prayer and study of the

Bible, I can learn the glorious truth that God is the All-Sufficient One. If I wait on His Spirit, God promises to help me in my need.

God really longs to bestow new things on those who pray to Him. Can I believe this today? Can I face the truth about myself and the real nature of God? Can I admit that I have character defects, but that God has none?

I need a deepening and soul-searching humility in my prayer life. As my self-confidence decreases, my God-confidence must increase, or I will become increasingly hopeless. God wants me to trust in His omnipotence. He wants me to pray with an increasing, believing boldness. He wants me to express my great need for deliverance in the faith that He will graciously save me from destruction.

PRAYER FOR TODAY

Dear Jesus, in my strength I did not know you; but, in my defects I have met you at the point of my greatest need. Today, give me the power to rest in your loving, caring arms.

5 | GOD'S POWER CAN FILL MY EMPTINESS

I pray also that the eyes of your heart may be enlightened in order that you may know . . . His incomparably great power for us who believe. That power is like the working of His mighty strength, which He exerted in Christ when He raised him from the dead. **(Ephesians 1:18, 19)**

No matter how powerless I feel, I need to remember that the almighty power of God will work within me.

God helps me accept the fact that I am powerless to overcome my addictions and dependencies; therefore, I can also accept that by His power I can change. God wants me to admit that I cannot control my own destiny, and then confess that He is the one person I can trust to rule my life.

If I will only believe in God's willingness to work in me, He will give me a daily share in the resurrection power of His Son. The resurrection of Jesus is connected with the wonder-working power of God. Such power God seeks to bestow upon me daily, if I will only admit my need of Him in prayer.

Each day, I need to confess my weakness and God's strength. Through this confession, I can have the confidence I need in the power of Jesus Christ to redeem me and restore my joy and peace. If I trust God in prayer, His power in Jesus will give me the victory when I am tempted.

In my fellowship with God, the Holy Spirit can fill me with the joy and victory won in the resurrection of Jesus Christ. When I pray in the midst of my temptations and trials, Jesus will give me the power to overcome. Let the cross of Jesus Christ humble me to death, so God can work in me by His Spirit.

PRAYER FOR TODAY

Dear Heavenly Father, I am so early into my recovery that I do not understand all you are trying to tell me about your power to overcome my addictions. I only see my failures. Even though I lack understanding, by your mighty Spirit work powerfully within me and set me free from every addiction, that I might grow in grace and comprehension for Jesus' sake.

The Second Step

Came to believe that a Power greater
than ourselves could restore
us to sanity.

---

*Because Jesus himself suffered when he was
tempted, he is able to help those who are being
tempted.* (Hebrews 2:18)

THE SECOND STEP

Came to believe that a Power greater than ourselves could restore us to sanity.

What strong, encouraging words I find in the Second Step: believe, power, and restore. Until I first believe, I will do nothing. But when I come to believe, I open the door of my mind to receive the power I need to change.

In the First Step, I discovered that belief can be painful. I painfully came to believe the truth about myself. Oh, how I hated to look at myself in the mirror. In the Second Step, I can joyfully believe and affirm that a Power greater than myself can heal my body, mind, and spirit. God restored the lives of many in my Fellowship when they turned themselves over to Him and sought His guidance. So, I have good reasons to prayerfully take this Step as well.

The Bible gives many examples of what God can accomplish in the lives of men and women who believe and follow Him. Those I meet in my Fellowship also tell many stories about how a Power greater than themselves saved them from insanity or certain death. As I believe and trust in God more and more, I will find great power in prayer—an almost miraculous, life-transforming power. But without faith, I can do nothing. From the Bible and the testimonies of people I meet, I can believe that God will do seemingly impossible things in my life too.

I need to learn what these words of Thomas Carlyle mean: "A man lives by believing something; not by debating and arguing about many things." Until I move beyond debating about the existence of God, about whether He loves me, and about how He expresses that love, I will not be restored to sanity. Debating is so close to rationalizing that I will not find healing until I put down my verbal weapons and believe. Then, I will make more progress in the Program. God will work great changes in me, until my life no longer contradicts what I am coming to believe.

6 | A CURE FOR MY ANXIETY

Do not be anxious about anything, but in everything, by prayer and petition, with thanksgiving, present your requests to God.
(Philippians 4:6)

Without God I am lost. I cannot concentrate on my real needs or overcome my problems. I cannot even pray. I try one thing and then another, but either I fail or they fail me. I used to keep picking myself up, but now I am sick and tired of falling over and over again. I need a Power greater than myself to give me healing and stability.

God, help me to believe that only a real, continuous companionship with you will help me. Show me how prayer can become a daily life activity—moment by moment. I want my dependence on my Higher Power to be just as natural as breathing or sleeping, not something I use just once or more a day like some drug.

I will follow the principle of completely depending on God for everything. I will develop the habit of remembering that He is present with me each moment of the day. Since God is always near, I may call upon Him at all times. Eventually, my experiences with God will teach me not to be anxious about anything.

I need to remember two things: God is always near with His infinite and abundant grace ready to overcome my problems. And, I am in utter frailty, and must call upon Him to give me the power I need. I want to give the holy, gracious God all the time I can, so His light, life, and love will fill my whole life. If I give Him time, through His Word and prayer, His love will abide in me.

PRAYER FOR TODAY

Dear God, sometimes I find it difficult to believe that you will help me. I have spurned your gracious offer of help for so long that I am not sure you will hear me now when I call. Yet, I have the testimony of others in my Fellowship, along with your Word, that you will help me. So, Lord, I am coming home.

7 OVERCOMING MY GREATEST STUMBLING BLOCK

Come to me, all you who are weary and burdened, and I will give you rest.
(Matthew 11:28)

My greatest stumbling block was the feeling that I could never change. Old habits, emotional attachments, and the attractions of my surroundings had a strong pull on me. Whenever I thought victory was out of reach, I also thought, Why try? Now I recognize that the change I needed was too difficult for me to make alone.

Each day, I need to ask God for the courage to believe that change and deliverance are possible for me. I need to ask Jesus for the courage to trust in Him, to ask Him to change me in any way He sees best.

A defective spiritual life will lead to a defective prayer life. O Jesus, free me from the power of sin, and give me a life of true faith and prayer! Give me victory over my unbelief, and then give me the courage and power to change.

Rather than follow the spirit of discouragement, I will place my faith in Jesus and choose to follow the spirit of gladness and hope.

God says, "Give yourself to me. Believe that I will help you pray. Believe that I will give you transforming power. I long to pour my love into your heart. Be conscious of your lack of power, and then rely upon me to give you grace and the power of prayer. I will cleanse you from all sin. I will deliver you from the sin of prayerlessness—only do not seek the victory in your own strength. Bow before me as one who expects everything from his Savior. However sad or discouraged you may be, be assured of this: I will be gracious and give you a believing heart; I will teach you how to pray and how to change."

PRAYER FOR TODAY

Dear Jesus, after trying so many ways to change and after saying so many prayers, I almost lost all hope. Once again I need to let go—O God, change me. Give me all the power I need to recover from my troubles. Begin the healing I need today. As I wait on you, give me your peace and assurance.

8 | JESUS MAKES ME NEW

Therefore, if anyone is in Christ, he is a new creation; the old has gone, the new has come! (2 Corinthians 5:17)

For a long time I felt I had given God and Jesus a chance but they had failed me. I was too impatient or too demanding or I expected too much too quickly.

I found that my whole approach to and relationship with Jesus, as my Lord and Savior, had to be entirely new.

First, I came to understand that because of His infinite love, Jesus really does seek to have communion with me every moment of the day. With all His heart, Jesus longs for me to enjoy His companionship.

Second, I came to believe in His divine power to conquer sin and keep me from falling. When I am tempted, if I look, I can find Him providing ways of escape for me and giving me the power I lacked to follow Him out of trouble. With greater frequency, I now look to Jesus in prayer when I feel overpowering temptations.

Third, since Jesus is the Great Intercessor, I now know that He will fill me with joy. Through the Holy Spirit, He will give me the power to have daily communion with God in prayer.

Fourth, I have discovered that when I awake each morning I need to come to Jesus and surrender to Him once again. He will make me new each day. Then, I ask Him to completely control my prayer life throughout the whole day.

My prayers are now becoming what God means them to be. Through the Spirit, my prayers are becoming the natural and joyful breathing of my spiritual life. In my communion with Jesus, I now inhale the heavenly atmosphere and exhale my prayers to God. What a joy when prayer and obedience become as natural as failing used to be!

Prayer for Today

Dear Jesus, take charge over me. Since you died for me, I can trust you and your love to guide me safely through life. Since you were raised from the dead for me, I know your power in me will be adequate for any situation. Teach me how to pray and remain in constant communion with you.

9 | MY POWER FROM ON HIGH

I am going to send you what my Father has promised; but stay in the city until you have been clothed with power from on high. **(Luke 24:49)**

Why does Jesus pay attention to powerless, helpless people like me? Because He knows that when I give Him the opportunity to rule as Lord in my heart He can show His power to overcome in all things.

In the lives of His disciples, Jesus proves that all power has been given to Him in heaven and on earth. When Jesus fills me with His Spirit, I cannot keep His power under my control. I must yield myself to the mighty power of God and allow Him to work in me. Like Christ on earth, my place is to pray, believe, and let the Holy Spirit work through me and in me.

I want Jesus to give me a prayerful attitude and an unceasing dependence upon Him. I need to pray daily with the confident expectation of receiving God's guidance and power in my life.

Jesus' first disciples saw Him love and heal the sick, cast out demons, and raise the dead. They saw His power over everything. They received His teaching and saw His sufferings. They saw Him in His power and in His seeming weakness. But in His weakness, they saw the power of God in His life. They saw Him raised from the dead, and they experienced His resurrection power in their hearts.

They also learned that without His living presence and power in their hearts each day they were not able to make the truth about Him known to others. From His throne in heaven, Jesus had to take possession of them by His Spirit and dwell within them.

Jesus longs to do the same in my life. All I need to do is maintain my daily, prayerful, obedient contact with Him.

PRAYER FOR TODAY

Dear Jesus, overcome my unbelief and skepticism. You are the Creator and Sustainer of all. Help me to rely on you in every situation. Help me to yield myself totally to you, so that I can know you personally as my Redeemer and Friend.

10 THE SECRET OF MY POWER IN PRAYER

If you love me, you will obey what I command. And I will ask the Father, and He will give you another Counselor to be with you forever. (John 14:15,16)

I will not be content with anything less than the indwelling life and power of the Holy Spirit in my heart. I cannot live reasonably and have the power to overcome my trials, troubles, and temptations without Jesus working in me each day. Through daily prayer, I can know He is with me and at work in my life.

If I want God to restore me to substantial wholeness, I need the same devotion to Jesus that I saw in His first disciples. The Lord Jesus asks this of everyone who desires to be filled with the power of His Spirit. God desires to fill me. Moreover, He wants me to receive His Spirit and power so that I can pray and intercede for others more effectively, to link my needs and the needs of others to the throne of God.

To some, Jesus is something or nothing. For those who do not know Him, Jesus is nothing.

For the average believer, Jesus is something. For me, Jesus is everything. To receive the power of the Holy Spirit, I need to pray each day: "Lord Jesus, I yield myself with my whole heart this day to the leading of the Holy Spirit." A full surrender, a total letting go and letting God, is a matter of life or death, sanity or insanity—an absolute necessity.

I have discovered that the mark of a true disciple is surrendering to God's love every day, all the day; abiding in the Lord Jesus and keeping His commandments with a total reliance on His power and strength to help me obey.

When I long to do God's will in everything, His love and Spirit rest upon me and give me peace. In this spirit, I always find my secret power in prayer.

PRAYER FOR TODAY

Dear God, I desperately need your power. I need you—not just now in this time of need, but every moment of the day. Teach me to pray and rely on your powerful presence in my life through Jesus' indwelling Spirit.

The Third Step

Made a decision to turn our will and
our lives over to the care of God, as
we understood Him.

---

*But he said to me, "My grace is sufficient for you,
for my power is made perfect in weakness."
Therefore I will boast all the more gladly about my
weaknesses, so that Christ's power may rest on me.*
(2 Corinthians 12:9)

THE THIRD STEP

Made a decision to turn our will and our lives over to the care of God, as we understood Him.

The key words in the Third Step are decision, turn, and care. Through the success stories of others in my Fellowship, and from the examples in the Bible and other books, I see what great and wonderful things God can accomplish in those who have yielded their lives to His care. Eventually, I also need to decide to let go of myself and let God take control. After all, who better understands my needs than the One who created me?

God created me with the ability to choose. Left alone or in rebellion against authority, I will make decisions that will destroy my life and hurt others. God, however, has the character, competence, and power to control my life in all matters. Therefore, to keep growing in His grace, I must turn my freedom to choose over to Him. I do this in prayer. From the heart I say to God, "I give up; you take over. Show me what to do and I'll do it."

Jesus said that God cares for the birds of the air and the flowers in the fields but that He cares much more for people. After all, He created people in His image. He cares for me now as I take these Steps; but I limit Him greatly if I continue to make choices contrary to my best interests. Only God knows what is best for me. He cares for me by showing me what is best.

If I limit my understanding of God to my own imagination or to the ideas of others, I may not trust in God to really care for me. Throughout my life things have happened that have tended to warp my ideas about God. Therefore, as I prayerfully read the Bible, and think about the ideas in the books I read, I need to pray and ask God to show me who He really is. As I learn more about who God is, I can go joyfully to God each day in prayer, grateful that He will care for me as I turn that day over to His care.

11 | TAKING TIME WITH GOD

There is a time for everything, and a season for every activity under heaven.
(Ecclesiastes 3:1)

God has designated a time for everything—so why don't I spend more time in the presence of my Creator? Why not take time to contemplate His will and purposes for me? Why not take time to measure my attitude and actions according to His revealed will in my reason, conscience, and the Bible?

My holy, loving God deserves the best of my time—of all my time. He merits the best in my life. I need to live in constant fellowship with God each day. To keep growing in faith, I must set aside a special time of quiet to be alone with God, to ask Him to examine and improve my life.

I need a daily period for private fellowship with God. I need a time for Him to shine the searchlight of His love into my heart, to reveal my hidden faults and intentions. I need time to turn daily from my occupations and search my heart in His presence. I need time to study His Word with reverence and godly fear. I need time to seek His face and ask Him to make himself known to me. I need time to wait until I know that He sees and hears me, so I can make my needs known to Him from the depth of my heart.

If I let God be God, and remember that I am only a creature, He will take the time to deal with my needs. He will assure me of His forgiveness, cleanse me, and fill me with His mighty Spirit.

PRAYER FOR TODAY

Dear Father, I am so inclined to put everyone and everything else before you. Almost habitually, I give you the time that I have left over, instead of putting you first and giving you my best time. Too often, the time I give you is at the close of a hectic day, when my mind is too exhausted to talk long with you. Help me to overcome these faults by showing me the benefits of time spent with you.

12 | WILLING GOD'S WILL

My Father, if it is possible, may this cup be taken from me. Yet not as I will, but as you will. (Matthew 26:39)

To abide in unbroken fellowship with Christ and maintain ceaseless prayer to God, I need to surrender my life to Him every day, give myself over to His care, and ask Him to help me die to sin and the world.

Only Jesus can teach me what it means to turn my life over to His care and also have fellowship with His sufferings. When He agonized in prayer on Gethsemane, and looked forward to His death on the cross, He got such a vision of what it meant to die an accursed death under the power of sin (with God's countenance so turned from Him that not a single ray of its light could penetrate the darkness) that He prayed the cup might pass from Him. But when He heard again the Father's will, He yielded up His whole will and life to God in the words "Your will be done."

With these same words, I can enter into fellowship with God. With these words, Christ makes my heart strong and gives me confidence to believe that God will enable me, with Christ, to yield up everything to Him, to be "crucified with Christ," to overcome my problems and inherit eternal life.

"Let God's will be done." May this bold declaration be the deepest and the highest word in my life. In the love of Christ and in the power of His Spirit, may this definite daily surrender to the will of God become the joy and strength of my life of prayerful obedience.

PRAYER FOR TODAY

Dear Jesus, help me see that I need more than just a little correction of the course my life has taken. Today, I give my life completely over to you for your guidance and protection. Daily, help me to stop living in a way that is destructive. Turn me to you so completely that I will be crucified with Christ each day and live in your power, wanting only your will for my life and the power to do it.

13 | FROM MY STRENGTH TO GOD'S

Blessed are those whose strength is in you, who have set their hearts on pilgrimage. They go from strength to strength, till each appears before God in Zion. (Psalm 84:5,7)

When I cling to God's promises in the Bible, He assures me of His unfailing love and faithfulness through Jesus my Lord.

When my growth through the Twelve Steps goes slowly, I thank God for the promises He has made to me. Through the indwelling Spirit, I go from strength to strength. The Word and Spirit assure me that God will perfect His work in me. Through daily prayer, I have learned to rely only upon God's grace.

God closely connected the Holy Spirit with our prayer life. After I received the Holy Spirit through prayer, I realized that a life in the Spirit requires continuous prayer. If I continually give myself to prayer, then I can be led continually by the Spirit. As I submit myself to the Spirit's control, I avoid destructive behavior and become a true blessing to others.

Am I willing to decide today to turn myself over to the care of God? Am I willing to reaffirm this decision daily? Am I willing to ask God to take control every time I want to follow my feelings and return to my old ways of living?

God wants to accomplish a great deal in my life, but my spending time in prayer and fellowship with God is an absolutely indispensable condition for God to work fully in my life. Jesus Christ revealed that if I open my heart and mouth toward heaven, He will not fail me or put me to shame.

To obtain God's blessings, I must pray. My heart must be entirely surrendered to Him, and I must believe in the power of prayer. I rest now with the assurance that God will care for me and work powerfully in me as I turn my life over to Him, and do so daily in prayer.

PRAYER FOR TODAY

Dear Father, if I limit you to my finite vision, I am too scared to turn my life over to you. As I pray and read your Word, give me faith to place my life in your hands and rest on your promises.

14 THE SPIRIT WILL PRAY FOR ME

In the same way, the Spirit helps us in our weakness. We do not know what we ought to pray for, but the Spirit himself intercedes for us with groans that words cannot express. (Romans 8:26)

If God left me to myself, I would not know how to pray. God stooped down and rescued me in my helplessness by giving me the Holy Spirit to pray for me. The work of the Holy Spirit in the believer's life is deeper than our thoughts or feelings. God hears the Spirit in our prayers in ways beyond our understanding.

The Holy Spirit teaches what the Bible means about God. The Holy Spirit works in us so we can turn our lives over to God and receive His care. The Holy Spirit helps us humbly admit that any recovery or progress we make is due to God's work in us.

Before I turned my life over to God, He worked upon me from the outside. Now, as a believer, the Spirit works with power from the inside.

From the inside, the Holy Spirit gives me power to change.

Because I have turned my life over to God, I can come into His presence with the confidence that the Holy Spirit's work will be carried out in my prayers. Such confidence will inspire reverence and quietness, and will enable me to depend on the Holy Spirit to present my needs and desires to God in a way that He will accept. Through the Holy Spirit, my prayers will have more value than I can imagine.

In every prayer of the believer, the Triune God participates. God the Father hears our prayers. We pray in the name of His Son, so He will answer our prayers. And the Holy Spirit prays in us and for us about the things we need. When we turn our lives over to the Triune God, we know that God will hear our prayers and meet our needs.

PRAYER FOR TODAY

Dear God, help me to believe in the reality of your Holy Spirit working in my life. Turn my attention from myself, so my heart will make room for your Holy Spirit to indwell.

15 | THANKING GOD FOR HIS CARE

And I will pour out on the house of David and the inhabitants of Jerusalem a spirit of grace and supplication. They will look on me, the one they have pierced, and they will mourn for Him as one mourns for an only child, and grieve bitterly for Him as one grieves for a firstborn son. (Zechariah 12:10)

I thank God for the certain promise that He will care for me now that I have turned my life over to Him. I reckon, with full assurance of faith, that through the Holy Spirit, God now indwells me as His Temple.

The Bible calls the Holy Spirit the "spirit of grace and supplication." He now dwells within me to rule; therefore, I have power to become a new person. I thank God when I pray, and ask His Spirit to fill me with more reasons to praise and thank God for His blessings. Thanksgiving in prayer draws my heart closer to God and keeps me consciously aware of His care.

Without prayer, I found the work of going

through the Twelve Steps too hard. At first, I tried to have fellowship with God as I imagined Him to be, but that did not work. I had tried to pray apart from the Holy Spirit. I found that communion with God was impossible to achieve without the Spirit's help.

The Holy Spirit reveals the Father and the Son to us, and glorifies the Son. When I turned my life over to the care of Jesus, the Holy Spirit made such changes in me that Jesus received all the praise and thanksgiving for my recovery. The Scriptures reveal that God wants Jesus to receive the glory and honor for my victories.

The Spirit of Holiness teaches me to recognize, hate and turn from evil. When I came to understand that the Holy Spirit is the Spirit of Wisdom, Love, and Power, I more readily committed myself to His daily guidance and care through prayer.

PRAYER FOR TODAY

Dear Father, thank you for the difference I have found in praying with the Holy Spirit, knowing He is the Spirit of Prayer. Continue caring for me by helping me to keep changing daily by your power as I pray in Jesus' name.

The Fourth Step

Made a searching and fearless moral
inventory of ourselves.

---

*Search me, O God, and know my heart; test me and
know my anxious thoughts. See if there is any offen-
sive way in me, and lead me in the way everlasting.*
(Psalm 139:23,24)

THE FOURTH STEP

Made a searching and fearless moral inventory of ourselves.

Almost everyone has spent a lot of time hiding from who he really is. In the Fourth Step, I will prayerfully ask God to search out those things in my life that have hurt Him, others, and myself.

My choices will be moral or immoral depending upon the intention of my heart—the main source of every person's actions. An action that flows from love for God and others is moral—though the right intention does not prevent someone from making a mistake. On the other hand, an action that flows from selfishness and self-centeredness is immoral—though sometimes a person may do a helpful thing by accident, or to get honor, praise, and glory from others (a wrong motive).

When I take a moral inventory, I will list both the right and wrong things I have said and done, giving close scrutiny to my motives. I can thank God for the good things. As I list each action, I need to ask myself, "Why did I do that?" As Bill W. often said, "In rationalizing, we often hide a bad intention under a good intention." I need to ask myself, "What is my ultimate intention for everything I do?" I can list good things I did from a wrong intention, perhaps things I did to manipulate others. And I can list mistakes I made from a good intention, and remind myself not to feel guilty for ignorant mistakes I could not help. I bear no guilt for mistakes made with a good motive, but I do bear guilt for the things I have done with a wrong motive, with a selfish intention.

A moral inventory or list needs to include things I *have done* and things I *have not done,* things I *could have done* and things I *should not have done* in my life. I can overcome my fears of such a searching by reminding myself that I am now under the care of a loving, heavenly Father who will forgive me, give me the courage to face myself, and empower me to change.

16 THE ROOT CAUSE OF MY PROBLEMS

If we claim to be without sin, we deceive ourselves and the truth is not in us.
(1 John 1:8)

I am searching for the root cause of my character defects and for any reasons within me for my problems. I need to direct my attention first to that, or secondary influences and problems will always plague me and I will never have the healing I seek.

Through prayer and meditation, God will give me proper insight into my true character. God will help me see myself as He sees me and others may see me. I need to stop fooling myself and misleading others. As I begin to list the wrongs I have done, I will overcome the deadness and failure I feel sometimes in my private prayers. As I begin to deal with my problems and their root cause, I will not blame my lack of fellowship with God on Him.

What is the root cause of my problems and my failure to hear from God? Is it selfishness and self-centeredness? Do most of my shortcomings have their origin in my obsessive self-concern? Have all of my prayers focused on the things I want from God and others? Oh God, help me to recognize this evil and forever renounce it. By your grace, help me put you first in my life, and make room in my heart for you and others.

Just two things are possible: walking with the Holy Spirit or following my selfish desires and feelings. Oh God, fill me with your Holy Spirit, so I will not fulfill the compulsions and desires that harm others or myself.

PRAYER FOR TODAY

Oh God, as I begin to list the wrongs I have done, show me their root cause in my self-centeredness. Father, by your grace, help me put the axe to that root and remove it completely. Then, dear Father, fill the hole left in my heart with your love and the personal presence of Jesus Christ. Dear Jesus, make my heart your throne, so selfishness will never take root and live there again.

17 | GOD REVEALS MY PROBLEMS THE BEST

But if we walk in the light, as He is in the light, we have fellowship with one another, and the blood of Jesus, His Son, purifies us from all sin. (1 John 1:7)

I need to recognize my character defects, if I am to understand more fully the grace of God and how His Son can help me. As I prayerfully read the Word of God, the Holy Spirit will shine His light, give me understanding, and apply God's Word to the defects in my life. The Bible will teach me how horrible sin and its consequences are, and this truth will motivate me to avoid it. Such daily, prayerful reading and asking God to point out my sins in the light of His Word takes courage that only the Holy Spirit can give me.

I thank God that the Holy Spirit will not show me all my defects at once. God will gently and lovingly show me only what He knows I can bear and deal with that day.

If others try to be the Holy Spirit for me, the pain and shame of admitting my character defects may be more than I can bear. If I try to take the moral inventory of others, I may influence them to avoid their pain and run away from their problems or return to destructive behaviors.

I am prayerfully working through the Fourth Step so God can gently show me my problems and give me His remedy. I cannot allow myself to think that daily sin is a necessity and cease to mourn over my sins. I will make spiritual progress only if I bring my actions before my conscious mind, evaluate them, and confess every transgression against God, others, and myself each day.

PRAYER FOR TODAY

O God, make my conscience tender. If I sin, break my heart. When I am tempted, bring my conscience to bear down upon me with its solemn warnings, so I won't sin against you. As I read your Word, write your Law of Love on my heart and give me the power to overcome my defects and do right.

18 | THE PROBLEM OF PRAYERLESSNESS

As for me, far be it from me that I should sin against the Lord by failing to pray for you. (1 Samuel 12:23)

The sin of prayerlessness can have a terrible effect. In saying my prayers, I can be prayerless. If I deceive myself and do not get better, I can begin to distrust God and prayer. Prayerlessness can be a hasty and superficial communion with God, a hurrying to get on with "more important things."

Just saying my prayers every day will not help me hate sin or give me the power to flee from temptations. Praying needs to be more than just saying words, the same words, over and over again. When I just "say" prayers, I give my hand over to Satan and his power.

As God's child, I am slowly learning more about prayer, and that nothing but hidden, humble, constant fellowship with God can teach me to hate sin as God wants me to hate it. As I open my hidden life to God, He will help me hate sin and give me the hope of overcoming my flaws.

Only by maintaining a constant nearness to the living Lord Jesus will He give me unceasing power to understand how to detest and conquer my character defects.

As God's Word and Spirit reveal my sins to me, I need to develop a deeper understanding of prayer and God's willingness to grant me pardon. As I look to Jesus and remember what it cost Him so I could be forgiven, purified and renewed, He gives me power and works out the victory over temptation that I need. He fills me with peace, the real peace of God within me.

I can never repay the Lord Jesus for His gift of love to me, but I can linger longer in His presence and express my love and gratitude with words of praise. As I praise Him, I will become more like Him and His holiness will rest upon me.

PRAYER FOR TODAY

Dear Father, as I list my flaws, help me see that these led Jesus to die on the cross for me. In the days ahead help me to spend more time with you as I pray longer over your Word.

19 | THE ONE WHO CAN SAVE ME

You are to give Him the name Jesus, because He will save His people from their sins. (Matthew 1:21)

As I list the things I have done to harm others and myself, I need to remember that the Lord Jesus will forgive me and save me from my transgressions. The name Jesus means Savior.

As His follower, Jesus wants me to love and adore Him each day. Have I done this? If not, have I put this on my list? Does my list include honoring or dishonoring God?

Through daily communion with Jesus, He will save me from my sins. He will reveal himself to me, and through the power of His love He will cast out my love for sin. He will save me from my trespasses by the power of a daily personal fellowship with Him.

To be saved from my sins, I need to bring my heart to Jesus, even with the sin that is in it, and ask Him to be my almighty personal Savior. He can save me from every sin in my moral inventory. As Jesus and I spend more time together and express our mutual love for one another, by the work of His Holy Spirit in my heart, His love will expel and conquer all sin within me.

I need to learn the blessedness of maintaining fellowship with Jesus each day. Communion with Jesus is the secret of all true happiness and holiness. As I do this more and more, my heart will long for the hour of prayer, because it will be the best hour of the day.

As I spend time alone with Jesus, I will experience His presence enabling me to love Him, serve Him, and walk in His ways. Through unbroken fellowship with a holy God, I will have the secret power of a truly holy life.

Prayer for Today

Dear Father, I find listing my sins one by one to be heart rending; but, as I do so I remember that you will forgive me for each one and that you can expel my love for any sin and help me conquer my addictions. Please give me the faith I need today to keep on working this Step.

20 | MY REASON FOR REJOICING

Jesus said, "Father, forgive them, for they do not know what they are doing. (Luke 23:34)

As I continue working on my moral inventory, I rejoice that God loves me in spite of what I have done. God loves His enemies as well as His friends. Just as Jesus prayed for His enemies as He hung on the cross, I know He is praying for me as I make a list of the wrongs I have done. He died for me. Now from heaven He intercedes for me with rejoicing as I complete this Step.

Jesus calls me to love my enemies too, to pray for them, and bless them. As I think of those who influenced me to do wrong, I am tempted to hold a grudge against them or even hate them. As I think about these people, I need to forgive them just as Jesus forgives me. Hanging on to old resentments will only hinder my spiritual growth and keep me from having the close communion with God that I need through prayer.

When I think of the repentant thief who prayed to Jesus for mercy as he hung upon the cross beside Him, I marvel at the wonderful love of God. I rejoice in Jesus' readiness to forgive and the joy He must have felt when He said, "I tell you the truth, today you will be with me in paradise" (Luke 23:43). I trust in God's ready forgiveness; this faith inspires me to keep on examining my life thoroughly.

The cross of Jesus is a cross of love. I owe my future to the sacrificial, redeeming love of God. As I pray to God and confess my errors and trespasses, I know that He will forgive me and enable me to follow Him more nearly each day.

Prayer for Today

Dear Jesus, the only thought that sustains me, as I look at my life with all the degrading things that I have done, is the certain knowledge of your willingness to forgive me, accept me, and give me a new life on earth and in heaven. Thank you for giving your life to forgive me.

The Fifth Step

Admitted to God, to ourselves, and to
another human being the exact nature
of our wrongs.

---

*Therefore confess your sins to each other and pray
for each other so that you may be healed. The
prayer of a righteous man is powerful and effective.*
(James 5:16)

THE FIFTH STEP

Admitted to God, to ourselves, and to another human being the exact nature of our wrongs.

As I list and admit my wrongs, I need to think about what influenced me to do those things. Did my family background or some great disappointment or tragedy influence me to take the path that led to my actions and addictions? Can I acknowledge these influences and at the same time accept the full responsibility for my past decisions and deeds? Can I remember the turning points or crossroads, when I deliberately made wrong choices—even if partially from ignorance?

All trespasses were conceived by Satan or other people to be addicting. If they weren't, how could such harmful indulgences be successfully advertised and kept on the market? Taking even one forbidden action can lead to bad habits and make it harder to say "no" to the next temptation. Thoughts and actions lead to the habits that form our character. Admitting my responsibility for the exact nature of my wrongs will lead to my spiritual, mental, and physical healing and the formation of the honorable character I seek.

As I take the Fifth Step, I need to remember that God's loving presence is with me—enfolding me with His loving arms and holding me so close that nothing I confess would ever lead Him to let me go. As I confess to God, He will console me as I have never been consoled before. As I confess each trespass, His Spirit in some mysterious way will heal my breaking heart. Because He once lived upon this earth as a man, Jesus understands everything I have ever done and will forgive everything I ever confess.

Through prayer for God's guidance in taking the Fifth Step, God can lead me to someone with the compassion and caring of Jesus to hear my confessions. If I confess my trespasses to someone with the Spirit of Jesus, he will forgive me and can even pray with me for the healing and strength that I will need for the future.

21 | CONSCIENCE AND CONFESSION

If we confess our sins, he is faithful and just and will forgive our sins and purify us from all unrighteousness. (1 John 1:9)

For my conscience to work as God intended, I must truly repent of the wrongs I have done. I must confess my outward actions (that I and others know about) and the hidden thoughts that have prompted me to act in ways that were harmful. To find happiness and wholeness, to be freed from the power of my blighted past, I must list and confess each individual sin and shortcoming by name. I must be intensely personal as I pray to God and ask His forgiveness.

How wonderful to think that a holy God invites me, an unworthy sinner, to come to Him for the assurance of forgiveness and fellowship. He invites me to come and experience the depth of companionship with Him that only the forgiven enjoy. He created me in His image and redeemed me by His Son, so I can have salvation from the power of sin and life ever lasting. How wonderful to realize that God has provided the solution to my every problem. Surely, God does not want any unconfessed sin to stand in the way of a blessed and glorious relationship with Him.

When I am sick, I try to discover the true cause of my illness and the best way to treat it. This is always a first step toward my recovery. The cause of many of my problems is the burden of the unconfessed sins that I carry. After I take the time to confess every sin, God has promised to cleanse me from all my corruptions. Then I will know that the smiling face of God is upon me when I pray.

PRAYER FOR TODAY

Dear Father, as I confess my sins and shortcomings, my defects of character, and the harm these have caused, show me everything that I must confess— when I am ready to remember them. Show me the gravity of my transgressions slowly; otherwise, I could not take the pain and go on. Cleanse me from my sins as I confess them so that I can know the joys of completing this Step as I go along.

22 | LIFE FOLLOWS DEATH TO SELF

Unless a kernel of wheat falls to the ground and dies, it remains only a single seed. But if it dies, it produces many seeds. (John 12:24)

Every seed teaches how I will receive a beautiful and fruitful life by dying to self. Confession kills pride and brings forth the beautiful fruit of humility. God gives grace to the humble. Jesus had to pass through death in all its bitterness and suffering before He could rise to heaven and impart His life to those He redeemed. So, I must die to the self-life.

When I admit my shortcomings to God and another human being, I die inside. However, the death of pride will lead me to new life, peace of mind, and the assurance of God's accepting and forgiving love.

I once wondered, "Did Jesus really need to die?" But so it was: God laid upon Him the evil deeds of us all and Jesus yielded to the Father so through His death we might have life. Jesus' death made our forgiveness and new life possible.

As I confess my inner bondage to many evil things, through my fellowship with Christ and His cross, I will die to my preoccupation with self and be freed to really live. My prayers will become God-centered instead of self-centered. With joy and eagerness, I will learn to obey His call to bear my cross and die daily. In every prayer, I will see myself as "crucified with Christ." Knowing that Jesus works within me will inspire me to gladly die daily the death to self that will bring me into fellowship with Him and give me new life.

The Spirit of Christ Jesus, the Risen Lord, can make His death and life my daily experience. In yielding submissive prayer, Jesus will give me power to overcome temptation and conquer every spiritual enemy.

PRAYER FOR TODAY

Dear Jesus, how humiliating to think of confessing my sins to you and another human being. Yet many in my Fellowship have told of the joy of sins forgiven and the new life they received from the confession of their faith and faults. Give me courage to do what seems impossible to me now.

23 | GOD'S FORGIVENESS INSPIRES MY LOVE

The LORD, the LORD, the compassionate and gracious God, slow to anger, abounding in love and faithfulness, maintaining love to thousands, and forgiving wickedness, rebellion, and sin. (Exodus 34:6,7)

Until a person really confesses his sins to God, he cannot understand how abundantly God forgives. Through confessing my sins, I will come to know by experience the riches of God's mercy. By His faithfulness and abounding love, God has led me to the point of being ready to admit to Him the exact nature of my wrongs. I cannot doubt that His compassion and grace are also able to forgive me and restore me to fellowship with Him. Confession will remove all the barriers between God and me, and my prayers will be completely unhindered. True confession leads to true communion.

Through understanding more of God's character, His hatred of sin and His love for humankind, the fact that He is holy yet slow to anger, I will come to love Him more. The secret of maintaining the openness with God that I seek is being willing to confess any sins I commit each day. As I confess my shortcomings and seek His cleansing from all unrighteousness, I will keep my heart clean. As I meet with God each day, I will live in the light of His love. I have learned the secret to success in prayer: I need to draw near to God with absolute surrender to His will and desire to know and walk in His ways each day.

When I know with assurance that God forgives and will forgive me when I admit my wrongs, I can approach the throne of grace with boldness. Completing the Fifth Step will go a long way in helping me learn more about effective prayer— prayer that receives the answer it seeks.

PRAYER FOR TODAY

Dear Lord, I once disobeyed your command to love you. But you reached out to me in the love of Jesus and forgave me. You opened the way for me to come into your presence and I fell in love with you. Fill me with your loving presence and do not let me go, so my love for you will grow each day.

24 GOD WILL FORGIVE MY PRAYERLESSNESS

But when you pray, go into your room, close the door and pray to your Father, who is unseen. Then your Father, who sees what is done in secret, will reward you. (Matthew 6:6)

No one other than God and the one who helps me take the Fifth Step need know the exact nature of my wrongs. But after I take the Fifth Step in secret, I will have the freeness and openness I have needed to pray to God in secret. As I spend more and more time with God, He will make such a difference in my life that others will openly see the rewards of working the Program and doing so in constant prayer and reliance on God.

The Lord Jesus, the one who saves us from our sins, is able and willing to deliver me from all sin. He will deliver me from the sin of prayerlessness and failing to spend time with Him in secret prayer. To experience this deliverance, I must acknowledge and confess in a childlike and simple way the sin of not using a private place of prayer. Almost all of my problems have come from failing to spend time with God and asking God to lead me, free me from evil, and empower me to do good. With deep sorrow and shame, I need to confess my failure to really spend quality time with God in prayer and meditation upon His Word.

I need to confess that I was deceived in thinking that I could solve my problems and get through life in my own strength. I need to confess that I thought I could pray as I ought without the help of the Holy Spirit. I need to confess that the power of the world and my self-confidence led me astray and that I do not have the strength to do better alone.

If I will confess these things with all my heart, God will give me wonderful success as I continue working this God-given Program.

PRAYER FOR TODAY

O God, lead me to a person who will understand these things, as I confess the great sin of not spending time in secret prayer with you.

25 | *My Forgiveness Brings Singing*

I acknowledged my sin to you and did not cover up my iniquity. I said, "I will confess my transgressions to the Lord"—and you forgave the guilt of my sin. (Psalm 32:5)

Confession can be superficial. Honest confession gives power over sin. In fellowship with the Lord Jesus I need to confess every sin with an open and sincere heart, for every sin will hinder victorious faith.

Once David was unwilling to confess his sins, but then he learned, "When I kept silent. . . your hand was heavy upon me" (Psalm 32:4). He also discovered that after confession God surrounded him with "songs of deliverance" (Psalm 32:7). When God chastens or disciplines me, He does so to save me now and forever from sin. When I return to God and confess, all heaven rejoices. Jesus said, "I tell you, there is rejoicing in the presence of the angels of God over one sinner who repents" (Luke 15:10). And, "I tell you that in the same way there is more rejoicing in heaven over one sinner who repents than over ninety-nine righteous persons who do not need to repent" (Luke 15:7). I cannot neglect taking this Step.

When I confess my sin with shame, I also hand it over to God. I trust God to take it away. Taking the Fifth Step reminds me that alone I am wholly unable to rid myself of my guilt. I must act in faith that God will deliver me through the precious promises Jesus has made to those who repent.

As I work through the Program, I will discover two truths by experience. First, I will know that my sins are forgiven. Second, I will learn that Jesus is cleansing me from my sins and keeping me from falling.

As I seek prayer fellowship with Jesus each day, I need not fear confessing each sin in the confident assurance that He will forgive and deliver me.

PRAYER FOR TODAY

Dear Jesus, I know you save your people from their sins. I believe in the great power I will find through confessing my sins because you have borne the great burden of sin. Thank you for being both my Lord and Savior, today and forever.

The Sixth Step

Were entirely ready to have God
remove all these defects of character.

---

*Wash away all my iniquity and cleanse me from all
my sin. For I know my transgressions, and my sin is
always before me. Restore to me the joy of your salvation and grant me a willing spirit, to sustain me.*
(Psalm 51:2,3,12)

THE SIXTH STEP

Were entirely ready to have God remove all these defects of character.

How wonderful to have the Twelve Steps to follow in just the right order! As I examined my life in the Fourth Step, I could be honest with myself and not worry about the future or about what I would do with what I discovered. After making my moral inventory, I began to concentrate on finding the right person with whom I would share my grief and guilt. After taking the Fifth Step, I felt such peace and release that I could look with real hope to the future and begin to think seriously about what actions I would take regarding my defects of character.

As I think about my addictions, I know I want these removed. I know how destructive they have been. As I think about my compulsive behaviors, I know I don't want to be a slave to these any longer. However, as I think about some of my dependencies, I am so comfortable in some that I wonder if I really want to give them up. And yet, if I am to be whole, unhealthy dependent relationships need to be changed. I need to pray for God to make me ready to have these dependencies transformed into new relationships or removed.

I also need to get rid of all the bad habits I cling to, habits that will eventually destroy my body and mind, even if I do rationalize that they are helping me cope right now with my feelings. Am I entirely ready to give up *all* my bad habits?

I will pray for God to strengthen me, so I will make a firm decision to have *all these defects of character removed*. Each Step I have taken has required me to make a decision. I know that God has been with me empowering me to make these decisions and take every action. I praise God for how far I have come in my recovery!

After taking the Sixth Step, I will have worked half the Program. As I look at the spiritual progress I have made, I know that with God's help I can work through the whole Program— one day at a time.

26 | GOD WILL REMOVE MY FEAR

He has raised up a horn of salvation . . . to rescue us from the hand of our enemies, and to enable us to serve him without fear in holiness and righteousness before him all our days. **(Luke 1:69,74,75)**

I am my own greatest enemy. My own character defects and shortcomings can cause me far greater harm than anyone else. But these need not ruin the rest of my life. God can remove them, and then fill the vacancies they leave with His holy presence. But am I ready to have God remove my defects of character? Or do I want to live with the continual fear that my actions may someday destroy me and others?

If I humbly bow before the Lord Jesus and ask Him to rule in my life, then He will remove all my shortcomings and fill me with His loving presence. Thank God for His promise of Jesus in me.

Through the Holy Spirit, Jesus will dwell in me and give me the power to keep from doing evil. Through Jesus abiding in me, I will have the desire and the power to do God's will in all things. Think of the inspired words of Zacharias, as he prophesied the deliverance that the Lord Jesus would bring: As we serve Him, we have no reason to fear Him. These are the words of God and they show what He will do for those who seek Him.

God's promises are sure and are fulfilled in those who wholeheartedly and confidently claim them from Him. "I will cleanse you from all your impurities and from all your idols. I will give you a new heart and put a new spirit in you . . . and move you to follow my decrees and be careful to keep my laws. *I the Lord have spoken, and I will do it*" (Ezekiel 18:25-27,36).

PRAYER FOR TODAY

Lord Jesus, help me to see deeply into my heart and admit that apart from you I can do nothing. Help me see you as you really are and my defects as they really are. Help me become entirely ready to have all my character defects removed. Help me cast off my favorite vices so I can be substantially whole and receive your promised presence.

27 | JESUS PROMISES TO TRANSFORM ME

Trust in God; trust also in me. You may ask me for anything in my name, and I will do it. (John 14:1,14)

When I receive Jesus as my Lord, God will grant me all the fullness of His redeeming grace. Through fellowship with Jesus, I will enjoy redemption day by day. A close, daily fellowship with Jesus will keep me from slipping back into my old ways. He makes it possible for me to persevere in a living, powerful, prayerful, life of obedience.

In Jesus, God promises to remove all my defects of character. In my morning prayers, I can begin and maintain an intimate, spiritual, personal and uninterrupted relationship with my Lord through the day. And He will manifest himself with great power in my life. In the Lord Jesus, all the attributes of God will work powerfully within me and morally transform me. When I ask Jesus to remove my character defects, He will do it. Then daily fellowship with Him in prayer will give me the power I need to overcome every temptation to return to my old destructive ways.

As the glorified Son of God, Jesus' presence can fill me at all times and give me the power I need to live a transformed life. As a disciple of Jesus I need to learn this lesson: "The Lord loves me so, that He wants me near Him continuously, so I can experience His love." Every time I feel powerless to change, I need to remind myself of His ever-present love for me and within me. Remembering this will give me power in prayer, as I pray for myself, those I love, and others in my Fellowship and church.

When I commit my life to the Lord for the whole day, His eternal, almighty power will protect me and accomplish every good thing. When I take time for prayer, I will experience in full reality the presence of almighty Jesus!

PRAYER FOR TODAY

Dear Jesus, in holy love, you sacrificed your life to conquer sin in me. Fill me with your love and give me an abiding sense of your presence so that I will be changed and be an example of your saving grace.

28 I CAN BECOME LIKE GOD

*I am the Lord your God; consecrate your-
selves and be holy, because I am holy.*
(Leviticus 11:44)

I need to learn how to give God's holiness the
place it needs in my faith and life. To practice
God's holy presence, I need to read God's Holy
Word as I pray.

In the Book of Leviticus, God commands five
times, "Be holy, for I am holy." And the Apostle
Paul writes, "May He strengthen your hearts so
that you will be blameless and holy in the presence of our God and Father when our Lord
Jesus comes with all His holy ones" (1
Thessalonians 3:13; 4:7; 5:24). God will make
me holy, like Him.

Only by knowing God as the Holy One will I
become holy. I will not obtain this knowledge of
God unless I spend some time alone with Him
in prayer. I need to take time and allow the holiness of God to shine on me.

How can anyone obtain intimate knowledge of a
person with extraordinary wisdom unless he

associates with that person and remains under his influence? Likewise, how can God make me holy if I will not take time to be brought under the power of His glory and holiness? Only through prayer and meditation upon the Word of God can I come under the power and influence of God and get to know His holiness. Someone has said, "No one can expect to make progress in holiness who is not often and long alone with God."

Holiness is the most profound word in the Bible. John heard the four living creatures call out: "Holy, holy, holy, is the Lord God Almighty" (Revelation 4:8). By simply thinking, reading, and hearing, I will not understand or partake in the holiness of God. I need to be alone with God and pray: "Let your holiness, O Lord, shine more and more into my heart that I may become holy like you."

PRAYER FOR TODAY

Dear Father, make me ready to have all of my character defects removed. Then, as I turn more of my life over to you, fill me with your holiness. By your Holy Spirit, transform my life daily so that my character will become more holy as you are holy.

29 RECEIVING THE FULLNESS OF GOD

Your attitude should be the same as that of Christ Jesus. **(Philippians 2:5)**

Because Jesus humbled himself and obeyed to the death, even death on a cross, His Father exalted Him. Above everything else, the obedient spirit of Jesus needs to become the chief characteristic of my disposition. I need to pray for Jesus' attitude toward life and death and ask Him to give me His viewpoint on everything.

As I prepare to ask God to really remove all of my character defects, am I also willing to obey God in all things? Could my major character defect turn out to be my unwillingness to try and obey God in everything? Am I willing to pray: "O God, help me always to do your will"?

An employee who habitually disobeyed his boss and hurt others would be fired. Likewise, as a child of God, I should not habitually disobey God. Should God treat me any differently from the way an employer would treat an employee out to do harm? If I repeatedly confessed the same trespasses and did not surrender to God and pray for Him to remove my character defects, how should I expect God to treat me?

The Holy Spirit desires to possess me fully. To receive the fullness of His loving presence, I need to fully surrender to His rule. The Scriptures command me to be led by the Spirit and walk by the Spirit. To have a right relationship to the Holy Spirit, I need to pray for His constant guidance and rule over my life. Obeying God from a heart full of love is the most important factor in my whole relationship to God.

It is one thing for me to want to be rid of those habits, addictions, compulsions, and dependencies that are destroying me, and quite another thing for me to be ready to obey God in all things. The difference means turning from self-centeredness to God-centeredness.

PRAYER FOR TODAY

Dear God, if I am not committed to fully obeying you, I will get confused by the conflicting "leadings" I may get in prayer. Help me to take seriously the meaning of this new Step in my Program of recovery.

30 PRAYER LEADS ME TO VICTORY

What a wretched man I am! Who will rescue me from this body of death? Thanks be to God—through Jesus Christ our Lord. (Romans 7:24,25)

My life has a mighty influence over my prayers. If I am worldly and self-seeking, my prayers will be powerless and unanswered. Is there a conflict between my life and prayer? Am I ready for God to make any changes He finds necessary so that my prayers will be more effective? Am I ready to have every character defect removed? Am I ready to avoid every situation and flee from every opportunity that will tempt me to do wrong?

I cannot allow the ways of the world to have the upper hand in my life. I need God to rule and exercise His mighty influence over me. Prayer can conquer sin. In prayer, I will yield myself completely to God. My entire life can be brought under the control of God through prayer. If I receive the Lord Jesus and the Holy Spirit into my life, then through prayer they will change and renew my life; they will purify and sanctify me.

If I am not ready for God to remove my character defects, the rest of my prayer life will be defective. I will be working myself up to pray more and more and will be disappointed at the results. Only as God strengthens my spiritual life, through my daily surrender to Him, will my prayer time joyfully increase. The way I live cannot be disconnected from the way I pray.

Which has more influence over me, a five-minute prayer or my worldly desires? If my prayer life and my desires contend with each other, then I may concentrate more on fulfilling my desires than obeying God. If I give God total control and surrender my heart to Him, then prayer will come to rule my life. After I ask God to take full possession of my heart and life, prayer will become as sacred and powerful as God wants it to be.

PRAYER FOR TODAY

Dear Father, make me willing to have you remove all of my character defects. Help me see that my future depends on taking this crucial Step.

The Seventh Step

Humbly asked Him to remove our shortcomings.

Ask and it will be given to you; seek and you will find; knock and the door will be opened to you. For everyone who asks receives; he who seeks finds; and to him who knocks, the door will be opened.
(Matthew 7:7,8)

THE SEVENTH STEP

Humbly asked Him to remove our short-comings.

As God leads me through the Twelve Steps, and I pray over and do whatever the Program requires, God makes me more humble. God has never embarrassed and will never embarrass me. Whereas my dependencies brought humiliation, God brings jubilation. God will never disgrace me; but, the destructive idols that I have served will always, eventually, degrade me. Chemicals or practices that promised me success and happiness have led to shortcomings that brought me so low I had to look up to see bottom. In desperation, I sought God. I now ask Him to remove my shortcomings and dependencies on anyone or anything other than God and His loving, infinite, merciful, forgiving, almighty power.

Following the Twelve Step Program will help me overcome the dishonor of abuse or abusing, and help me live without arrogance. I will no longer live tooting my own horn for fear no one else will. After God removes my shortcomings, people will see me treating them more courteously and respectfully. They will know by the changes in me that I have been spending more and more time with a redeeming and transforming God. God alone will receive all the credit for my recovery as I humbly praise Him publicly and privately for His work in overcoming my defects.

The Sixth Step led me *to be ready* for God to remove my shortcomings. Now in the Seventh Step, I will turn to God and *ask God to remove them all*. As I pray, I will need to be specific in my requests. My *specific prayers* will show God that I understand my shortcomings and know these flaws are not just slips but real character defects that God alone can remove. I will confess that I have either been unwilling or unable to overcome certain habits and practices, and that I now want God to take over my entire life and conquer certain individual defects that concern me.

As God gives me victory over some of my shortcomings, I know He will prevail over them all. I need to surrender daily to God, asking God for power *for that day* to do His will in all things. I thank God for the triumph over temptation and sin that He has promised through faith in Jesus.

31 | GOD'S WONDERFUL PROMISES TO ME

For I will forgive their wickedness and will remember their sins no more. (Hebrews 8:12)

The Lord Jesus died to atone for my sins. By His grace through faith, He will destroy the power of sin over my life. He came to give me free access to God's presence. So in His name I can secure God's favor when I pray. He came to remove my shortcomings and give me a new heart. He freed me from the power of sin and filled me with the Holy Spirit. The Spirit now breathes in me the power to obey God in all things.

I will put my trust in Jesus for the forgiveness of my sins and claim the fullness of His other promise—that He will remove all my shortcomings. Not only will He remove them, but He will cleanse me and give me such a delight in and love for God's law that I will rejoice in God's commandments. God will give me such power in prayer that I will focus more on Him and others instead of merely on my own problems.

I have come a long way from breaking the rules and ignoring the consequences. I now see why all of God's standards are right and reasonable. I need Him to remove my defects of character so I can do right. If I ask Him, Jesus will write God's law on my heart by the power of His Spirit so I will know how to act in every situation.

God asked Abraham, "Is anything too hard for the Lord?" (Genesis 18:14). If I will set aside my preconceived opinions and believe in the almighty power of God and His desire to help me, He will remove my shortcomings.

PRAYER FOR TODAY

Dear Father, help me remember that my forgiveness and the removal of my sins (as far as the East is from the West) came at the cost of your Son's life. Because He suffered and died in my place, I am certain that He is willing to live in me and overcome all my shortcomings. Thank you God, for all the promises in your Word that I am just beginning to understand.

32 | GOD WILL WORK WONDERS IN ME

I pray that out of His glorious riches He may strengthen you with power through His Spirit in your inner being, so that Christ may dwell in your hearts through faith. (Ephesians 3:16,17)

Only the God who works wonders can help me. If I ask Him in faith, He will remove all my shortcomings. If I lack love, I can go to the throne of grace and He will fill me with love. Whatever I really need He will see that I have.

The gift of love only comes when Jesus fills my heart with His presence. As I seek God daily in prayer, Jesus will sustain my love for Him. As Jesus dwells more fully in me, He will lovingly remove all my shortcomings. When I humbly bow before the throne of grace, wait, and worship there, I will receive the indwelling Spirit and know the love of Christ.

I do not seek forgiveness only; I also seek that abundant grace that will help me to be continually victorious over sin and temptation. During my time in prayer and meditation on the Word of God, I ask God to fit me for the continual indwelling and guidance of the Holy Spirit. I earnestly pray that I may so live that the love of Christ that passes all understanding will be first place in my life. Only by spending time before the throne of grace will I be rooted and grounded in the almighty love of God.

When I have come to really love God and have gotten beyond just talking about my need to love Him, His love will radiate from me to all those around. Even those who do not yet love Him will be reached and enriched in their hearts by the love of Christ in me.

By faith and through prayer I will obtain the state of blessedness I seek.

PRAYER FOR TODAY

Dear Father, strengthen my faith according to the riches of your glory. Show me more of your wonder-working power by removing my shortcomings so that I can know more of the love of Christ and love others as I ought.

33 GOD'S LOVE WILL REMOVE MY HATRED

My command is this: Love each other as I have loved you. (John 15:12)

Jesus' command to love is so difficult to keep that I am often tempted to quit trying. Some have done some very hateful things to me and others. Yet, the Twelve Step Program requires that I recognize my own hateful attitudes as shortcomings and character defects that need to be removed with God's help.

As Jesus loves me, His love comes to fill me. As I open more of my heart to Him, He will fill me more and more. As He dwells within me, He casts out my character defects—if I humbly ask Him. Day by day through prayer and asking Him to remove these destructive attitudes, compulsions, and feelings, I find myself improving and learning to pray even for my enemies. As I spend more time with Jesus, I gradually begin to take on His loving and forgiving character.

If I say I love God and hate my brother, I am a liar. If I hate my fellow man, this is a sure sign that I do not truly love God.

Jesus really means, "Love each other *as I have loved you.*" Through the Holy Spirit, that He sends to live in every believer, He will enable me to love others. As I love others in the power of Jesus' love, they will also grow strong in love. As they grow strong in love, I will have powerful evidence that Jesus dwells in me and the Father has filled my heart with His love.

I want to bow at the throne of Jesus; and love, worship, and adore Him for His wonderful grace. By His love, He seeks to transform me and make me more like himself. As He lives in my heart, He will cast out all hatred, give me a wonderful love for others, and prove to the world that God is definitely in our midst.

PRAYER FOR TODAY

Dear Jesus, help me see that my biggest character defect may be my attitude toward others. Help me to see those I despise as you see them, with your compassionate desire that everyone be transformed by you into your image.

34 MY WHOLE LIFE DEPENDS ON JESUS

Trust in God; trust also in me. (John 14:1)

Jesus taught His disciples to pray to and believe in Him with the same perfect confidence they had in God.

I need to ask God to remove those flaws that influence me to visualize a god compatible with my character defects. If I think of a god with defects instead of the perfect God, I am more comfortable; but if I am to really change for the better, I need to ask God to remake me into His moral image—into the perfect image of His Son.

The deity of Jesus is the rock upon which my faith depends. The Lord Jesus, as a man, partook of my nature, but without any defects of character or moral flaws—He lived without sin. He is indeed true God. Just as divine power raised Jesus from the dead, so His divine omnipotence can work in me all that I need.

I need to humbly ask Jesus to remove any defects in me that keep me from seeing God as He is. Jesus said, "Blessed are the pure in heart for they will see God" (Matthew 5:8). As Jesus removes my flaws and creates a pure heart within me, I will see God as He really is, and I will take time to bow before Jesus and worship Him as I worship the Father.

I need to be conscious of Jesus' presence as my Redeemer, who is able to save me from my sins, cleanse me, and empower me to do right.

As I seek Jesus daily, I will come to love Him as the Mighty God and place all my confidence in Him as my strength. I need to ask Jesus to give me a direct, definite, unceasing faith in His power at work in me. As I rely more upon Him to remake my soul, He will show me all that He can do to transform my life.

PRAYER FOR TODAY

Dear Jesus, when so many say that you were just a good teacher, help me to see you as you really are. Reveal to me what flesh and blood can never reveal—that you are the Christ, the Son of the living God.

35 I Know God Will Help Me

Now faith is being sure of what we hope for and certain of what we do not see.
(Hebrews 11:1)

God will not remove all of my character defects all at once. He will usually remove them slowly and only one defect at a time. Their slow removal can encourage my steady spiritual growth and keep me relying daily on God for absolutely everything. Jesus trained His disciples to expect delay sometimes when they prayed. And He encouraged them to keep on trusting in God and persevering in prayer until His mighty power brought them the answer they needed.

When the answers to my prayers do not come according to my timing, the promises I firmly trust can appear to be false. In the trial of "unanswered prayer," I need to patiently wait on God. Through patience in times of trial, God will purify and strengthen my faith. By faith, I need to take and hold the promises of God until I receive the fulfillment of all that God promises in His Word.

God requires persevering prayer. Jesus taught that if an unfriendly, selfish friend would give someone what he needed when he kept asking, then God would do more, because God is an unselfish, loving, Heavenly Father. When God delays in giving me what I need, He is teaching me to live with Him in undoubting faith and trust—to indeed be His friend and not just want what He has to give. God may delay in removing my shortcomings, but by His grace and through trusting prayer each day, He will remove them.

Jesus did not promise to heal my every physical disease, but He did promise to save me from my sins. As I go to Him each day, I need to tell Him specifically the character flaws that I want Him to remove, and then by faith begin thanking Him for their removal. As the Spirit of Jesus works in me, I will see myself growing in obedience and gaining power over the temptations that once had absolute power over me.

PRAYER FOR TODAY

Dear Jesus, keep me patient when I wait in prayer. I have much that needs improvement. Work in me and make me into the person you want me to be.

The Eighth Step

Made a list of all persons we had harmed and became willing to make amends to them all.

Zacchaeus stood up and said to the Lord, "Look, Lord! Here and now I give half of my possessions to the poor, and if I have cheated anybody out of anything, I will pay back four times the amount." Jesus said to him, "Today salvation has come to this house." (Luke 19:8,9)

THE EIGHTH STEP

Made a list of all persons we had harmed and became willing to make amends to them all.

The first seven Steps helped me get right with God and daily prayer helps me stay right. Through daily prayer God shows me new and wonderful possibilities for living and His aims for all of my personal relationships.

I thank God for not requiring me to make everything right with others before coming to make things right with Him. God knows that without getting things right with Him first and without getting His guidance and help I can never really begin to make things right with others. I need to be willing to make amends to those I have harmed; but, first things first.

Once I am right with God, I will have God's help in restoring a right relationship with others where possible or advisable. By working the Eighth Step, I will explore how to heal relationships, how to make restitution, and the possible acceptance or rejection of my amends. As I think of all the new beginnings I have made with others almost incidently as I have worked through the first seven Steps of this Program, I am encouraged to press ahead with the Eighth.

Through prayer, God will help me remember and list all the persons I have harmed. I will expand my moral inventory as I focus my attention on the needs and hurts of others instead of on my own needs and pains. Working the Eighth Step will broaden my circle of concern beyond God and myself.

Through prayer, God will help me be *willing* to heal relationships. Every time I become willing to make amends, I have an answer to my prayers for that person and my attitude toward them. And I will pray differently for these, as I seek to learn whether or how I can make amends to them.

Becoming *willing* to make amends makes me deal with my deepest feelings of shame and disappointment. After I have become *willing* to make amends, I am set free. Almost miraculously I have overcome the fearful anticipation of seeing those I have hurt.

36 | SOME BENEFITS OF MAKING AMENDS

A new commandment I give you: Love one another. As I have loved you, so must you love one another. (John 13:34)

Jesus did not need to make amends to anyone for anything He ever did. He never did anything to harm God or humankind. In some mysterious way, however, when He died on the cross, He made amends for me in ways that I could never do. I could spend the rest of my life trying to make everything right with God and others and repair all the damage that I have ever done; but, I would never be able to get completely right with God and others—or live in the present for the future.

Being *willing* to make amends to everyone is a part of my recovery for spiritual and psychological reasons that only those who have taken the Eighth Step can begin to understand. I found freedom from guilt and resentment, from blaming others for my mistakes, and I began to take responsibility for my life in a more mature way. I found that things no longer hung over my head.

As I become more like Jesus and begin to love others as He loves me, I become more willing to make amends wherever I can. I begin to pray for and seek ways to restore broken friendships and relationships. Where I have not yet found a way to make amends with some, I begin to pray for God to bless them. My prayers become more concerned for the welfare of others and how I can make up with them or bless them and not just further my own recovery.

Jesus' command insures me of His power to carry it out. If I ask Him, God will always give me the power to do His will. Otherwise, God will often let me fail in my own strength to teach me dependence on Him.

PRAYER FOR TODAY

Dear Jesus, dwell in my heart with your divine love. Teach me to love others at all times and in all circumstances. You are the Vine and I am the branch. Give me the love I need for those I have offended, and make me willing to make amends.

37 | FORGIVING HELPS ME MAKE AMENDS

And when you stand praying, if you hold anything against anyone, forgive him, so that your Father in heaven may forgive you your sins. (Mark 11:25)

I am tempted to rationalize and keep resenting some people for what they did to me without accepting any responsibility for my own actions. These people are the very last I will think about with regard to making amends. Indeed, I may feel they need to make amends to me and hold a grudge against them until they do.

Realizing how I feel about some who have offended me motivates me to think about how I can make amends to everyone I have offended. I sometimes find it difficult to forgive those who have hurt me if they don't first seek to make amends to me. But there must be some I can help by going to them and seeking their forgiveness.

Refusing to forgive others, whether they try to make amends or not, and refusing to seek the forgiveness of others, will interfere with my prayers and recovery. As I become more and more willing to do God's will in this matter, He will give me greater freedom in prayer.

Jesus' love in me motivates me to seek the happiness of others—especially those I have harmed in any way. My hurtful words or actions may be keeping some from coming to God. Making amends may be the answer to their prayers and restore their confidence in God. If I make amends, some may see the love God has for them and come to believe in God.

Jesus saved me from my addictions not just to make me happy. That was only the beginning. Jesus wants me to share His love in words and in the heavenly power of His love in my life.

PRAYER FOR TODAY

Dear Jesus, as I pray, forgiving others, pour your love into my life so I will be able to bless those I have offended in any way by making amends to them.

38 | *I Will Take Up My Cross*

Anyone who does not take his cross and follow me is not worthy of me. Whoever finds his life will lose it, and whoever loses his life for my sake will find it. **(Matthew 10:38, 39)**

The Eighth Step leads me to even greater humility than when I took my moral inventory in Step Four. Now I need to be willing to face the people I have wronged, confess my shortcomings to them, and offer to make things right if I can. This will be especially difficult if I believe they have also wronged me and are undeserving of my amends. I need to pray for God to give me the willingness to complete this Step.

As a believer in Jesus, almost every Step requires me to take up my cross and follow Him. Every Step requires more of my self-life to die so God can live in and rule my life. When I pick up my cross to make amends, I die to self-pleasing and self-exaltation, and God gives me additional inner peace, power, and happiness. Each time I die to self, I find it easier to pray; because, I am becoming more like my heavenly Friend and Companion.

The cross is an instrument of execution: I need the death of my self-centeredness. Until I die to self, I will not humble myself enough to make amends to those I may have harmed who do not suspect my shortcomings. I may not need to make amends to them directly, or I may need to be anonymous as I make amends. But right now, I only need to pray for God to make me willing to make amends. I know that after I have taken this Step, God will also give me the wisdom and the power to take the next one—one day at a time.

PRAYER FOR TODAY

Dear Father, many of the truths I have been learning from the Twelve Steps, the teachings of Jesus, and those in my Fellowship are like little seeds. Make them germinate in my heart and reveal their full meaning to my mind. Make me ready to hear, understand, and obey your truth fully.

39 | WILLING TO GIVE UP EVERYTHING

In the same way, any of you who does not give up everything he has cannot be my disciple. (Luke 14:33)

Jesus does not require me to take a vow of poverty and live off others or welfare to be His disciple. Indeed, many who have come to know Jesus, or who have worked the Program, have overcome poverty and the need to depend on others instead of God.

Jesus does not want me to consider my possessions as my own, but as gifts from God to be used to bless others as well as myself. I am not to be self-centered or selfish when I see the needs of others, but ask God how or if I can help them.

The Program requires that I become willing to make amends to those I have wronged. This may require giving back something I have stolen, or returning money I have acquired by dishonest or unethical means. After I have given back all that I possess to God, it will be easier for me to accept the idea of making restitution wherever God shows me the need to do this.

Jesus Christ claims all from me; then, He undertakes to satisfy my every need and to give a hundred times more than I give up. This may not always mean material blessings, but it does mean spiritual satisfaction. As I thank God for the many blessings each renunciation of my self brings, I know that through my Higher Power my spiritual life will improve.

As I learn what it means to believe Christ is my life, I will count all things as loss for the excellency of knowing Jesus Christ as my Lord. In the path of following and loving Him, I shall be willing to sacrifice all to make room in my life for the One who is more than all.

PRAYER FOR TODAY

Dear Jesus, come into my life and enrich my immortal spirit. Help me to consider everything I have surrendered for you as my highest privilege instead of a burdensome obligation.

40 | WILLING TO FACE WHAT I LACK

Jesus looked at him and loved him. "One thing you lack," he said. "Go, sell everything you have and give to the poor, and you will have treasure in heaven. Then come, follow me." (Mark 10:21)

If my recovery seems to be slow, perhaps I am having difficulty facing all that the Eighth Step requires. In the depth of my heart, I need to become willing to make amends, and I need to look honestly at what that may require. Am I willing to sacrifice my prestige, power, or position to make things right with those I have offended, especially if this may come at great personal cost? I may not have "hit bottom" before beginning my recovery, so completing the Eighth and Ninth Steps may be particularly difficult for me. Yet, if I do not keep working the Program—one day at a time—I know I could fall back into my destructive compulsions.

By myself, I cannot complete the Eighth Step. Thank God my Higher Power will give me the strength I need to go on. Jesus promised, "all things are possible with God" (Mark 10:27). The Eighth Step reveals how much I need God for my recovery, to make me willing to sacrifice myself or my possessions to restore in some way what I have destroyed.

When Peter confessed Jesus as Lord, Jesus declared that he could only do that by divine teaching and the power of God. Only by divine power will I be able to accept what the Eighth Step requires. I need to pray daily for God to give me the willingness to do whatever He wants, and the wisdom to see what He requires. No one has ever naturally completed the Eighth Step without the help of God.

Some have sought to work the Program or follow Christ without seeking God's power through prayer, and they have failed. Some have felt that the Program was beyond their reach and have given up, without realizing that they needed their Higher Power to enable to do all that the Program requires.

PRAYER FOR TODAY

Dear God, help me put my trust in you as the living God who is willing to work in my heart to make me willing to do your will.

The Ninth Step

Made direct amends to such people
wherever possible, except when to do
so would injure them or others.

---

*If he has done you any wrong or owes you anything,
charge it to me. I, Paul, am writing with my own
hand, I will pay it back—not to mention that you
owe me your very self.* (Philemon 1:18,19)

THE NINTH STEP

Made direct amends to such people wherever possible, except when to do so would injure them or others.

I will not make amends to every person on my list, because as I work the Ninth Step I will recognize when making actual amends could be harmful and should be avoided. Certainly, I would not want to say or do anything that would hurt another while trying to heal my relationship with someone else. And I would not want to reestablish a destructive or unhealthy relationship. I need to pray for God's constant guidance as I complete this Step.

Since my life will not end at death, I can pray that when I reach heaven, God will heal my relationship with those who know Him too—the ones I could not reach here. But by waiting till I get to heaven, I do not want to avoid what God knows I can do here.

As I make my "amends list," I need to include those who have hurt me. I need to forgive them from my heart (as an act of my will) before I seek to make amends to them. Otherwise, anger or hidden resentments may interfere with the healing we both need. Eventually, good feelings follow good decisions.

Making amends may involve learning to love my enemies. God does not require me to have a warm glow of affection or fuzzy feeling for my enemies. But God does want me to pray and truly want the very best for them. I can pray that they will fulfill the necessary conditions for them to receive God's blessings. I may need to pray for them to work this Program.

I remember how difficult I thought taking the Fifth Step would be—talking to another person about my shortcomings. But the release and joy I experienced afterward made it all worthwhile.

Completing the Ninth Step restores a balanced mind and a balanced relationship with others. I will have peace with God, peace with others (at least within my ability), and peace of mind. With true peace, I will not return to destructive behaviors or addictions to escape my problems or achieve a false tranquility.

41 | *I Will Avoid Making Excuses*

Do everything without complaining or arguing, so that you may become blameless and pure, children of God without fault in a crooked and depraved generation, in which you shine like stars in the universe.
(Philippians 2:14,15)

As my learning increases from working this Program, I may be tempted to once again put my limited judgment over God's infinite wisdom. I may begin to think that I do not need to take the Ninth Step. I can imagine all sorts of scenarios that will give me reasons to skip it and move on. I might think my recovery has gone so well that I can drop out now and everything will still be okay. If I rely on myself to move on in the Steps, instead of my Higher Power, I will not complete the Program and will hinder my recovery.

I need to be careful and not rationalize that I would only hurt others by taking this Step. This may simply be my way of avoiding something I anticipate will make me uncomfortable or increase my pain. Have I really completed Step Eight; have I become willing to make amends to everyone?

The question may be one of pride in human wisdom and achievement. I need to remind myself again and again that humility is the key to my recovery. With humility, I need to go to God in prayer and confess my absolute dependence on Him for taking this Step. I need the Holy Spirit to teach me why the Ninth Step is so important, to give me the power to complete it, and to show me exactly the person or people I must make amends to.

In this Step, I will learn to rely on God day by day and moment by moment. I will pray without ceasing for the right attitude, actions, and words as I make amends.

PRAYER FOR TODAY

O God, open the way for me to make amends to those who will benefit from my efforts rather than be harmed. Keep me from hypocrisy as I complete this Step. As I make amends, may others receive me in a way that will bring healing, joy, and peace to everyone.

42 | THE HOLY SPIRIT WILL HELP ME

He will bring glory to me by taking from what is mine and making it known to you. (John 16:14)

I can receive the gift of the Holy Spirit through faith in Jesus Christ. When I follow Christ, the Spirit flows like a river within me. The Spirit flows from the Lord Jesus and reveals and imparts Him to me. Jesus sent the Holy Spirit from heaven so He could be glorified in the heart of every believer.

The fullness of God dwelt in Jesus Christ in order for Christ, as the life of God, to dwell in His followers. All the life and love that the Spirit imparts is in Christ Jesus. My whole spiritual life consists in union with Him. Each new day, I need to praise God that Jesus lives in me and ask Him to make His presence an abiding reality in my life. I need to rely upon the unseen working of the Holy Spirit in my heart.

With Jesus Christ living in me, I can impart something of His divine life and love to others as I make amends. Some will see the love of

Christ shining forth in me. I will glorify God as people see that my making amends comes from the spiritual renewal Jesus Christ is making in my life.

Some people will understand that my attempts to make things right with them indicate the progress I am making in this Program. These people will receive me with an open and forgiving heart. If they can also see that my making amends comes from the work of God in me, they will glorify God, and the Holy Spirit will continue keeping me humble when I do right.

In the life and words of His disciples, antagonistic leaders recognized that they had been with Jesus. As I spend daily time with Christ, the Holy Spirit will allow those I fear most to see God living and working in me.

PRAYER FOR TODAY

Oh God, help me overcome all my fears of making amends with those I can. Give me success as I reach out in love to do so.

43 | WHEN CHRIST IS MY LIFE

When Christ, who is your life, appears, then you also will appear with him in glory.
(Colossians 3:4)

Many believe that Jesus died on the cross for them and now lives in heaven. But few believe and live as though Jesus Christ lives within them. The powerlessness of many is mainly due to this narrow view. Do I really believe that the Almighty Lord *dwells within me*?

Believing that Jesus lives in me and is my hope for glory will free me to make amends without fearing the consequences. Through daily prayer, Christ will give me the direction and power to make amends in the best way possible. I will not simply say, "Jesus died for me, so my sins are forgiven," and then ignore making things right with those I have harmed. No. I will say, "Jesus died for me and now lives in me to overcome sin; therefore, by His power I will remedy the harm I have caused."

I need to know, experience, and testify to the truth that Christ lives in me. I cannot use my new found faith as an excuse for not righting wrongs wherever I can. Jesus lives in me so I can pray to know what is right and have the power to do it.

As others receive my offer to restore what I destroyed, they may see that these efforts flow from my desire to live wholly for God in Christ Jesus. Perhaps I can tell them that my efforts to make things right with them comes from my desire to have an abiding fellowship with Christ Jesus and do His will in all things. Taking the Ninth Step may give me the opportunity to take the Twelfth.

PRAYER FOR TODAY

Dear Jesus, some think Christianity is only an excuse to avoid accountability. Help me show that with you I am now more responsible than ever. Help me show that you want me to make things right wherever I can.

44 | PRAYER HELPS IN MAKING AMENDS

Pray in the Spirit on all occasions with all kinds of prayers and requests. With this in mind, be alert and always keep on praying for all the saints. (Ephesians 6:18)

I will not be alone and powerless to make amends when others in my Fellowship pray for me as I take the Ninth Step. I can ask those close to me to pray—pray for those I must speak to and pray God prepares me to say and do the right things with the right timing. In the Program, making amends does not need to be done alone. We can give prayer support to one another.

Thank God for this wonder of grace: we can pray down heavenly gifts upon one another. Making the effort to make amends may be the most difficult and responsible action I have ever taken. With God preparing the way and granting me success within as I make the attempt, I know that He will empower me to do all the Program requires.

I need to pray for others as they make amends. If I say I will pray for them, I need to pray right then for the success of their efforts.

The Program only requires that I make amends where possible and where it will not hurt others. God will show me how to avoid hurting others, either by not making amends or by not making amends the wrong way. The Ninth Step shows me how much I need to depend on God for everything.

If I cannot make amends personally, I can pray for God to make amends for me. God can restore to others what I cannot restore. God can bless those I have hurt. But I cannot allow prayer to be the substitute for whatever God wants me to do in personal action.

PRAYER FOR TODAY

O God, help me to be a real partner with others who are working the Ninth Step. Help me find some who will pray with me and advise me. Thank you for not leaving me alone to work this Program.

45 I WILL NOT GIVE UP

Jesus told His disciples...that they should always pray and not give up. (Luke 18:1)

One drawback in praying for God's guidance in making amends is delay. I will sometimes experience delay in receiving God's leading for specific people. This should not surprise me. I need to remember that God is preparing me to make amends and preparing others to receive my efforts.

God may have good reasons for delaying His answers to my prayers. My desire to make amends will grow deeper and stronger as I pray daily for the ones I need to reach. My love for them will grow as God's Spirit leads me in prayer. In God's timing, others will see God's love for them in me.

God has put me into a school of prayer: every delay teaches me to keep praying and not give up. As I persevere in prayer, God strengthens my faith. I need to believe that God has a great blessing for me and others from delayed answers.

Above all, God wants to draw me into a closer fellowship with himself. When my answers are delayed, I learn that nearness to God and love of God are more important than receiving the answers to my petitions—so I continue in prayer.

I need to remember the blessing Jacob received when his answer was delayed. He eventually saw God face to face. As a prince, he had power with God and prevailed (see Genesis 32:28-30).

I must not become impatient or discouraged when the answer does not come; but I must continue in prayer. I can ask myself if my prayer is according to the will and Word of God. I can ask myself if my prayer is in the right spirit and in the name of Jesus Christ. I can ask myself if I have really forgiven others. If I persevere in prayer, God will teach me what I need to do to secure His answer.

PRAYER FOR TODAY

Dear Jesus, help me to plead your promises and persevere in prayer so that I can have great power with God to achieve blessings for others as well as myself.

The Tenth Step

Continued to take personal inventory
and when we were wrong, promptly
admitted it.

*Search me, O God, and know my heart; test me and
know my anxious thoughts. See if there is any offen-
sive way in me, and lead me in the way everlasting.*
(Psalm 139:23, 24)

THE TENTH STEP

Continued to take personal inventory and when we were wrong, promptly admitted it.

The Lord's Prayer reminds me to seek forgiveness and forgive others daily. The Bible also teaches me to review my attitudes, actions, thoughts, and words each day.

Working the Tenth Step faithfully teaches me to be concerned about one day at a time. Facing my defects squarely, on a daily basis, ensures my continuing sanity, serenity, and spiritual growth.

As I work this Step, I need to read the Scriptures and pray for God to reveal any wrongs that I have overlooked since taking the Fifth Step. Through such prayer and meditation, I will develop a tender conscience and be open to the daily leading of God's Spirit. Then I will avoid doing wrong or more quickly confess any wrongs I commit. Working the Tenth Step will help me eliminate destructive habits and speed up my recovery.

Following this Program as a believer in Christ will help me evaluate myself according to valid, objective, and God-given standards. If my ethical standards differ from God's, then I will be tempted to justify behaviors that destroy others and myself. God's Word helps me and others solve that problem.

I need to humbly and promptly admit any violations of God's moral law. I will pray for God to help me do all things from the pure motive of love for God and others.

As I grow closer to the holy God, I will become more like God. And God will show me things I did not see when I took my Fifth Step. As He reveals these things to me, I will promptly admit these wrongs and pray for Him to help me do better.

I thank Jesus for dying for me. I know that God will forgive me for all my wrongs as I work this Program with a sincere and open heart.

46 REASONS FOR LACK OF PRAYER

Do not think of yourself more highly than you ought, but rather think of yourself with sober judgment, in accordance with the measure of faith God has given you.
(Romans 12:3)

I must not consider my circumstances a good excuse for my lack of prayer. God's Word tells me to look in my heart for the real reasons.

Sometimes I still feel hostility toward God and do not want to be with Him. Sometimes I still refuse to yield entirely to the Holy Spirit's leading. Sometimes I am still afraid to let go and let God take total control of my life. Before I realize it, my emotions have taken control of me.

I need to take a daily personal inventory. I need to check for these indications that I may be stepping backwards:

- Have I been too hasty in my words and actions?

- Has anger been arising unexpectedly within me?

- Do I sense a lack of love for God and others?

- Do I derive too much pleasure in eating and drinking?
- Has my conscience been accusing me of misbehavior?
- Have I been seeking my own will and honor?
- Have I been putting too much confidence in my own power and wisdom?

Reasons for a lack of quiet time and prayer can be traced to answering any of these questions with a "yes."

I am to live in the Spirit; but, sometimes I refuse to walk in the Spirit. When I recognize any of the above symptoms, I must ask God to forgive me, free me from the defects, and once again fill me with His love. By His grace, God will give me the power to pray and joyfully seek His fellowship each day.

PRAYER FOR TODAY

Dear God, help me to walk in faith and in the power of your Holy Spirit rather than follow my feelings. Whether I feel like praying or spending time with you or not, please help me to do so anyway. Show me what I lack and what you can overcome. Give me that joyful fellowship I really want and must have with you.

47 OVERCOMING SATAN

For our struggle is not against flesh and blood, but against the rulers, against the authorities, against the powers of this dark world and against the spiritual forces of evil in the heavenly realms. (Ephesians 6:12)

I must remember that Satan will always be my enemy. He wants to destroy my life and will use every weapon at his disposal. But thank God, through the weapon of prayer, Satan can be defeated. No wonder Satan will do his best to take this weapon from my hands or try to keep me from using it.

Satan will tempt me to postpone prayer or shorten my time in prayer. He will influence my thoughts to wander and bring distractions into my mind. Sometimes he can sway me toward unbelief and hopelessness.

But I can overcome Satan and return to happiness when I hold fast and keep using my weapon of prayer against all obstacles. When our Lord was in Gethsemane, as Satan attacked more viciously, He prayed more fervently. I can do the same. Jesus prayed and did not cease until He rose victorious. I can follow His example.

Without daily prayer and self-examination, Satan can quickly gain a foothold in my life. I must pray, for without prayer, the helmet of salvation, the shield of faith, and the Sword of the Spirit (which is God's Word), I will be powerless to defend myself and defeat my spiritual foes (see Ephesians 6:13-18). All depends on God and His promises. Persevering prayer enables Him to fulfill these quickly. May God be gracious and teach me to believe in Him and the power of daily prayer.

PRAYER FOR TODAY

Dear God, give me the power to persevere in prayer. Help me to see clearly all my enemies so that my prayers can be directed toward them. Keep me from blaming others if they bear no responsibility. Keep me from accusing myself if I bear no blame. Don't let Satan deceive me; but, let me see exactly what he is doing so I can use prayer wisely and according to your Word.

48 I TRAIN WITH A GOAL

Everyone who competes in the games goes into strict training...Therefore I do not run like a man running aimlessly.
(1 Corinthians 9:25, 26)

With the Twelve Step Program I am bringing order into my life. I am learning to work the Steps each day. Sometimes, I have slipped back into old attitudes and behaviors and have said and done things that have hurt others and myself. When this has happened, I have needed to promptly admit my wrongs and make amends where necessary; otherwise, the loss of my serenity has often led me to worse thoughts, words, and actions.

I need to remember I am in strict training for a spiritual goal. I need to give up everything that might be harmful to my spiritual growth. My daily, personal inventory needs to reveal what things I need to change as a part of my training.

Jesus wants me to have an undivided heart. He does not want me to strive for earthly prizes and glory as though these were more important than the heavenly. Have I been spending more time preparing myself for earthly success and accolades than I have for eternal rewards?

The Apostle Paul would not let anything deter him from pressing toward the mark for the prize. No self-pleasing in eating and drinking. No comfort or ease kept him for a moment from showing the spirit of the cross in his daily life. No thought of self kept him from sacrificing his all for his Master. Likewise, the cross needs to be the goal of my life.

O God, give me the spirit of the cross through the power of the Holy Spirit. When the death of Christ works in me, His life will be known to others through me. Jesus humbled himself and became obedient unto death on the cross. O Jesus, give me this attitude. Show me daily what I need to do to pick up my cross and follow you.

PRAYER FOR TODAY

Dear God, help me evaluate my life in the light of the cross each day so that I will never rest satisfied with my spiritual, material, physical, or mental attainments.

49   ABIDING IN CHRIST

We always carry around in our body the death of Jesus, so that the life of Jesus may also be revealed in our body...So then, death is at work in us, but life is at work in you. (2 Corinthians 4:10,12)

As I pray through these Steps and continue my recovery, I see new heights to reach. Things I never thought of as wrong before now seem horrible. As the Holy Spirit works within me, He shows me things to remove that are incompatible with His full presence in my life. But most importantly, He wants me to be Christ-centered instead of me-centered.

As I spend more time in prayer, I am learning the meaning of abiding in Christ. At first, this meant to me simply affirming His presence with me each day. Now, I am learning that it also means abiding in the crucified Christ. Once, I thought I only had to affirm once and for all, "I am crucified with Christ." Now, I see that I am to abide daily in the fellowship of His death by taking the form of a servant.

Jesus humbled himself and became obedient unto death—this mind of Christ needs to be the spirit that marks my daily life. However, I need to pray that as I become more Christ-like that I do not sustain or return to destructive, co-dependent relationships. The Holy Spirit will give me wisdom as I pray for His daily light in applying the Scriptures.

I am called to *always carry around in my body the dying of Jesus.* I am to live for the welfare of others. As I suffer with Christ, the crucified Lord can work out His life through me to help others. Am I doing this each day? Am I willing to do this? Am I willing for my self-centeredness to die so a new Christ-centeredness will live?

PRAYER FOR TODAY

Dear God, through my daily inventory help me consider these higher states of spiritual life. Help me remember that my wrong deeds do have a relationship to my life and death in Christ Jesus. Help me to die to self so that Christ may live in me.

50 | I Died on Christ's Cross

[Christ] himself bore our sins in his body on the tree, so that we might die to sin and live for righteousness; by His wounds you have been healed. (1 Peter 2:24)

If I do not keep my eyes on Jesus, I can become discouraged and think there is no hope for me. The things I hate doing I seem to do over and over again. I don't know how God can forgive me unless I remember that Jesus bore my sins in His body on the tree.

I will not be able to live unto righteousness unless I know that I have died to sin. The Holy Spirit needs to make my death to sin in Christ such a reality that I know myself to be forever free from its power. I need to yield myself completely to God, ask Him to forgive me, and make me an instrument of righteousness.

It has not been easy for me to comprehend what it means to die to sin and live to righteousness. But, dying with Christ on His cross remains the key to victory over sin and temptation. By God's grace through faith, I actually shared with

Christ in His death. To understand this will require self-sacrifice and earnest prayer. It will cost me a whole-hearted surrender to God and His will. It will require abiding and unceasing fellowship with the crucified Christ.

If these things have not been my heart's desire, am I willing to recognize these as shortcomings? Or, do I prefer to live on the level of law and morality instead of stepping up to the heights of a new spirituality?

As I pray through these Steps, resolving to live in full obedience to God, the Holy Spirit will show me the secret of dying with Christ to live fully in God.

PRAYER FOR TODAY

Holy Spirit, burn into my heart the meaning of having died to sin with Christ on the cross and set me forever free from its dominion. As I trust you daily, give me power over every temptation and keep sin from reigning over me for Jesus sake.

The Eleventh Step

Sought through prayer and meditation to improve our conscious contact with God, as we understood Him, praying only for knowledge of His will for us and the power to carry that out.

For physical training is of some value, but godliness has value for all things, holding promise for both the present life and the life to come. (1 Timothy 4:8)

THE ELEVENTH STEP

Sought through prayer and meditation to improve our conscious contact with God as we understood Him, praying only for knowledge of His will for us and power to carry that out.

The Program lets me contact God and understand Him for myself. The Program gives me complete freedom of religion, because it tries not to be specifically religious. Its primary concern is recovery from addictions, compulsions, codependent relationships, emotional disorders, and other shortcomings in this life.

Since many philosophies and religions teach different and often contradictory things about God and eternity, they cannot all be teaching what is real about God. Having come this far in my recovery, and having a clearer head and purer intentions, I now have the opportunity to discover more about my Higher Power as I work Step Eleven.

The Christian faith teaches some things from the Bible that almost every church and denomination proclaims to be of central importance. By using the Bible as my standard and thinking about what the Church has taught for centuries, I can come to accept some solid truths that will help me now and forever. As I study the Bible, Christian literature, and listen to other Christians, God will teach me more about himself—if I seek the knowledge of God's will only and the power to carry it out.

The Bible teaches me to meditate on its teachings and how to apply them. The scriptures teach God's will and way for all humankind. For example, I can meditate on the Lord's Prayer by thinking about ways I can "hallow," honor, show respect for, and teach others about God's Name. Or, I can thank God for all the names He applied to himself in the Bible so I could know a lot more about Him.

Christian meditation will turn me from self to God and God's way for my life. Such meditation will also protect me from following powers and guides that will deceive and eventually destroy me.

Through working the Eleventh Step, I have found out by experience that my recovery goes better when I seek first the will of God and His power for my life.

51 TRUE PRAYER LEADS TO TRUE FELLOWSHIP

To them God has chosen to make known among the Gentiles the glorious riches of this mystery, which is Christ in you, the hope of glory. (Colossians 1:27)

True prayer gives me contact with God. As I seek the holiness of God by persistent prayer, God covers my sinfulness with His holiness. As I get to know God better, my understanding of His greatness and power makes me more humble.

True prayer leads me to see that I can have fellowship with God only if I choose the road of humility. When Jesus becomes my daily example and guide in prayer, I truly live in Christ, just as Christ lives in the Father.

Above everything, true prayer consists of fellowship with God. Through daily contact with God, He possesses me and stamps my entire personality with the lowliness of His Son. In friendship with my Redeemer, I find the secret of true love.

In Jesus Christ I draw near to God. I have died with Christ, so Christ can reign in my life. By the power of the Holy Spirit, I need to affirm with assurance, "Christ lives in me."

Praying to the Father in the name of Jesus causes me to experience new joys and gives me greater power in prayer. I pray that God will strengthen me and encourage me to believe in the certain victory He will bring. Through true prayer I can receive blessings that are greater than I could imagine. God will do this for all who love Him, so I pray for Him to keep my love constant and sincere.

I have found that daily victory in prayer does not come immediately or all at once. God's fatherly patience continues toward me: He bears with His children. I rejoice in the promises I find in God's Word. And, as my faith grows stronger through prayer, I will persevere to the end and enjoy victory over my self.

PRAYER FOR TODAY

Dear Jesus, I feel my spirit thriving through daily prayer. Make me ever more willing to be humble or humbled, so I can always enjoy sweet communion with you.

52 | GOD WILL NOT FORSAKE ME

Those who know your name will trust in you, for you, LORD, have never forsaken those who seek you. (Psalm 9:10)

The Holy Spirit wants more of me. The Spirit of God wants to possess me entirely. Just as my soul indwells my body, so my body can serve me, the Holy Spirit wants to fully indwell my body and soul so that I can serve God. God wants His dwelling entirely under His control.

Until I have learned to trust God fully, I will not be ready for this new Step. As God demonstrates His love and faithfulness to me daily, He will overcome my fear of giving Him such total control of my life. Such total commitment will result naturally if I go to God in prayerful surrender each day to His care.

As I work through the Twelve Steps with reliance on God, the Holy Spirit will gently lead me to renew consecrations to God. The Spirit will inspire me to seek more of God in my personal experience. The Holy Spirit will show me how Jesus Christ will deliver me from all of my character defects and never forsake me. Jesus Christ, the Almighty Deliverer, comes near to defend me and draw me nearer to God. The Holy Spirit will lead me in my prayers for deliverance until I find the victory.

The Spirit of God will help me forget myself and seek more of God in prayer. Eventually He will make me willing to put my needs aside so that He can train me to intercede for others. The Holy Spirit will make me willing to trust God to carry out His plans for my life and for those who are important to me.

Prayer for Today

Oh God, draw near and help me to know the Holy Spirit more fully. Make me conscious of the work you want to do in me, for me, and others.

53 | I Am Crucified to Overcome

I have been crucified with Christ and I no longer live, but Christ lives in me. The life I live in the body, I live by faith in the Son of God, who loved me and gave himself for me. (Galatians 2:20)

As I have tried to work the Twelve Steps in the light of the Scriptures, I have found the lesson of the cross the most difficult to learn.

Jesus said "Take my yoke upon you and learn from me, for I am gentle and humble in heart, and you will find rest for your souls. For my yoke is easy and my burden is light" (Matthew 11:29,30). Through the love of Christ on the cross I am drawn to Him and receive His promise to help me bear my cross each day.

Love makes many things easier. I need to meditate day and night on His love for me until the Holy Spirit gives me personal assurance of His love and daily help in all my struggles.

I need the Holy Spirit to breathe into my heart daily, "You are a child of God." When I remember that the blood of Jesus washed away my sins, I have proof that God will never reject me—His child. Through the power of Jesus' shed blood I am well-pleasing to God.

As I seek to know God's will, I also need to see myself as a ruler and intercessor (king and priest) in Jesus' name. God will strengthen me through His power; then, I can conquer my character defects, overcome my temptations, and be filled with courage and joy.

God will also encourage me to intercede for others each day as I seek His will for my life. Through my prayers, others will more easily discover God's will for them.

PRAYER FOR TODAY

Dear Jesus, I will not learn in Twelve Steps over a few months what you have taught others over years. Teach me more as I reach up to learn from your Word.

54 REASONS FOR EFFECTIVE PRAYER

The prayer of a righteous man is powerful and effective. (James 5:16)

Prayer avails much with God. The history of His people proves it. Prayer is the one great power I can exercise to secure the working of God's almighty power in my life and the world.

The prayer of a righteous person is powerful and effective. This means the person whose righteousness is in Christ—not simply as a garment covering the person, but as an indwelling life-power in a person made new by Christ.

As I seek God, His will for my life, and His power to obey day by day, I will be what the Scriptures call "an instrument of righteousness" (Romans 6:13). My true joy and effectiveness in prayer will depend on my relying daily on the righteousness of Christ working in me. As I surrender to God, I will be more useful each day.

On the night before He died, Jesus gave His wonderful prayer promises to those who obey: "If you love me, you will obey what I command.

And I will ask the Father, and he will give you another Counselor" (John 14:15,16); and "If you remain in me and my words remain in you, ask whatever you wish, and it will be given you. If you obey my command, you will remain in my love" (John 15:7,10). Jesus promised that if I practice the Eleventh Step in His name, my prayers will be effective.

Only when a righteous person rouses his whole being to take hold of God will prayer avail much. The effective, fervent prayers of righteous people effect great things.

Wherever two or three righteous people agree in His name, Jesus has promised to answer their prayers.

As I continue to work the Program, may I see the importance of how I live my life in Christ before and after I pray in Christ. If my prayers are not effective, maybe I need to go back and work through some of the earlier Steps once again.

PRAYER FOR TODAY

Dear Lord, help me each day to live up to all the truth I am learning so that I can claim your promises in my prayers.

55 | REASONS FOR DAILY PRAYER

Give us each day our daily bread. (Luke 11:3)

Once, I was afraid to pledge that I would pray to God each day. I thought such a demand and commitment was altogether beyond me. And then, I discovered that I did pray each day for daily bread.

Surely, I should count it a privilege to come into His presence with my every need and the great needs of others each day.

Do I still desire to live wholly for God? Jesus Christ gave himself for me. His love now watches over me and works in me daily without ceasing. I will welcome the opportunity the Eleventh Step gives me to prove day by day that I am devoting my heart's strength to the interests of God's kingdom. I will rejoice in the honor of being asked to bring down God's blessings through daily prayer and meditation.

The Eleventh Step reminds me to call out to God each day for His power. My needs and the needs of others cannot be met without the promise of God's power. As I praise God for what His power has done for me and others in my Fellowship, I am amazed at what He has enabled us to carry out.

I have found great freedom and wonderful healing as I have worked the Program with others who have problems similar to mine. I will find great power and be more effective in prayer as God unites me with those who know Him as I do through Jesus. Surely, this must be a part of my seeking God's will for my life.

PRAYER FOR TODAY

Dear Jesus, help those who still hesitate to work this Step with a total commitment; help them to see the difference such a commitment has made in the lives of others. Help me to find others I can unite with in prayer to promote your Program and your redeeming love.

The Twelfth Step

Having had a spiritual awakening as the result of these Steps, we tried to carry this message to others, and to practice these principles in all our affairs.

Jesus said to them, "Go into all the world and preach the good news to all creation. (Mark 16:15)

THE TWELFTH STEP

Having had a spiritual awakening as the result of these Steps, we tried to carry this message to others, and to practice these principles in all our affairs.

Whenever newcomers show up at one of my meetings, I need to pray that God will help me welcome them in the right spirit and with the right words. With an open heart and mind, I will need to welcome them in such a way that they will be able to see what the Program has done for me. With the help of God, I will be able to encourage them by sharing what the Program promises and how my Higher Power has helped me apply and live by the Steps I have taken.

Through prayer and meditation, God will show me when I am ready to share the Program with outsiders. Having experienced a spiritual awakening, I will have substance and not theory to share with those who need to begin living the Program. If I begin to teach others about the Twelve Steps without praying for God to lead me, this may actually hinder my recovery or keep someone else out of the Program.

Perhaps the best evidence for others that the Program works will be my practice of the Steps in all my affairs. Having recovered substantially from my addictions, compulsions, obsessions, depressions, codependencies, and fears, I can now work out the Twelve Steps in all of my relationships. I can quit trying to control my wife or husband, parents or children, boss or employees. I can release them to the care of God. I can admit that I am powerless to rule their lives. I do not need to take their daily moral inventory to make myself feel better. I can let go and let God direct all my affairs and relationships and give me the power to work the right Step whenever needed.

As I pray daily and meditate on the Word of God, I will grow in my knowledge of God and be able to tell others more about Him and how He saved me. If others see I am not like the hypocritical, so-called "believers" they have known, perhaps God will get the glory for my recovery and they will be open to receive His help in theirs.

56 | THE POWER OF INTERCESSION

We are therefore Christ's ambassadors, as though God were making His appeal through us. We implore you on Christ's behalf: Be reconciled to God.
(2 Corinthians 5:20)

Let me consecrate myself to interceding more for others. The Apostle Paul wrote of praying for those he had not even met. Though personally limited by time and space, in the Spirit he had power in the name of Jesus Christ to pray for a blessing on those who had not yet heard of the Savior.

Let me pray each day for those who need to find God and deliverance, whether I know them personally or not. I can pray for the opportunity to tell them about God and a Program that will free them from their bondage to destructive thinking and injurious actions. I can pray for God to give me just the right words to share with every needy person He brings across my path.

Paul lived a heavenly life of love and amazing power in prayer. God will give me this same power if I will free myself from prayerless living. I need to pray that Jesus Christ will bring down a blessing on those who need God and free them from despair, discouragement, fear, pride, or other problems.

Imagine what would happen if more of us in the Program would pray for others. If I prayed more (privately and with others), it would make a wonderful difference in the number of people I could help.

PRAYER FOR TODAY

Dear Lord, help me to be more concerned about others now that my life has changed so much. Help me to keep working the Steps that I need. Lead me to others who need the type of help that I have been prepared to give through the Program you have given.

57 | GOD CALLS ME TO TELL OTHERS

You will be my witnesses. (Acts 1:8)

Since I have worked through the Program and come to know my Savior more personally through prayer, I am now ready to point others to the Person and Program that can work for them.

Jesus called His servants to witness for Him, to testify to His wonderful love and power to redeem. He called His servants to tell others about His continual abiding presence and wonderful ability to work miracles in their lives. Indeed, my spiritual awakening and recovery one day at a time qualifies as a miracle; especially when I look back and see what God has done through prayer. To witness, I simply need to tell what God and this Program have done for me.

Witnessing is the only outward weapon the King allows His redeemed ones to use. Without claiming special authority or power, without worldly wisdom or eloquent speech, without social status or privilege, *I need to be a living proof and witness of what Jesus can do.* In this way,

I do not point with pride to myself, but humbly to Jesus as my Higher Power.

Not by my words only, but by my transformed life, others will be brought to the feet of Jesus for salvation. When the first disciples were filled with the Holy Spirit, they began to speak of the mighty things Jesus had done. I can pray for the same Spirit to help others find the open secret that I have discovered through my spiritual awakening.

In the power of the Spirit, the disciples helped others in the name of Jesus. Filled with the life and love of Jesus, they spoke of what Jesus had done for them and this gave the good news power to help others. Here we have the secret of a flourishing spiritual fellowship: every believer witnessing for Jesus and what He does.

PRAYER FOR TODAY

Lord Jesus, please give me the strength, courage, and humility to be a transparent witness in helping others. Help me find one of my highest joys in telling others about you and a Program that works.

58 | WHAT MAY SET ME APART

The Spirit of truth who goes out from the Father, he will testify about me. And you also must testify, for you have been with me from the beginning. (John 15:26, 27)

Some have found help and sanity from sources other than the Program I have followed. Some view their Higher Power differently from me. I have learned not to proudly separate myself from them or look down upon them, but thank God for them and what He is doing in their lives.

In working the Twelfth Step, I will tell others about what God and the Program have done for me, then let go and let God go to work. My prayers for courage to speak will help me, but my prayers for those I tell about God and the Program will help even more—I can pray for others when I cannot be with them.

What may separate me from others in my Fellowship is the great truth that the Lord Jesus saved me and helped me with my recovery. I will be saying that my spiritual awakening involved a new relationship with Jesus Christ. My telling about the Program will be similar to the first disciples: they ceased not in every house to teach and to preach Jesus Christ. My Higher Power is Jesus. I am not ashamed to say so, even though my loyalty to Him may set me apart from others. If this happens, I will pray that others see the sweet Spirit of Jesus in me and not the condemning arrogance or judgmental attitude they have sometimes seen in others.

God cleansed me to serve Him. Through the Program, when I was powerless, God restored me to sanity. Today, I find my life is creative, joyful, peaceful, and full of God's love. I have an everlasting hope that I will see the Lord of Glory. God taught me how to pray and gave me His Spirit to teach me the Scriptures. God gave me a spiritual fellowship and a message to share. I have much and more for which to thank God.

PRAYER FOR TODAY

Lord Jesus, thank you for saving me. Give me the courage to tell the full truth about my recovery and the work of your Spirit in my life.

59 | My Personal Testimony

After they had prayed, they were all filled with the Holy Spirit and spoke the word of God boldly. All the believers were one in heart and mind. (Acts 4:31, 32)

What I share with others about my recovery needs to be based on my personal experience with God, prayer, and the Program. I can show others the Jesus of the Bible; but, showing them Jesus in my life may be more effective at first. By the grace of God, my recovery and restoration to sanity, one day at a time, will show what Jesus can do and not what I have done. But above all, I need to stay personal. Those who need the Program have heard enough theories. They need to see what works and the One who works.

The Holy Spirit will show what Jesus and the Program can do as people look into my heart. If I rely on Jesus and ask Him to live His life daily through me, they may see the loving work of God in my life. I need to pray that I can walk in such fellowship with Jesus Christ that He can reveal himself through me. Only the Holy Spirit can lead me and others to understand the indispensable secret of spiritual health—prayer in daily fellowship, childlike love, and true consecration to the Father and the Son.

I cannot fake a true spiritual awakening. Others will see through falsehood, to the discredit of Jesus, the Program, and me. I cannot allow myself to fall back into kidding myself by faking some spiritual trip. I need to pray that spiritual truths will be revealed to me personally by the Holy Spirit in some small way each day—for my sake and the sake of others.

PRAYER FOR TODAY

Dear Father, unite me with others of like heart and mind— those who know you personally and the power of your Holy Spirit in working the Twelve Steps. Teach us to pray together so your power might spiritually awaken other needy souls.

60 MY FUTURE WORK: CARRYING THE MESSAGE

"Come, follow me," Jesus said, "and I will make you fishers of men. (Matthew 4:9)

The Lord Jesus now expects me to help others find fellowship with Him in recovery. Since I have found a Higher Power and a Program that works and motivates me, I can carry the message to others more effectively. A part of my continuing recovery will depend on whether or not I remain God-centered and seek to share my testimony with others. I cannot allow myself to slip back into self-absorption and self-centeredness.

I have discovered the reason the Twelve Step Program works so well: it has been patterned after the teachings of Jesus and the Bible. The Twelfth Step teaches those in recovery what God's Word teaches all Christians about their duty: it instructs us to pray for and help others.

When I keep my heart right with God, I have freedom in definite, believing prayer and may expect God to bless my outreach to others. Having worked through the Twelve Steps, I understand the message so well that I can carry the message to others. But, I need to remember to rely daily on God to prepare the way for others to learn about the Program.

The health of my Fellowship group can be preserved only as those who benefit share the truths they are learning. The value of the Twelfth Step will be seen clearly when every member works this Step faithfully. Everywhere I look there are people who need help. I cannot always expect someone else to do the work.

My success in carrying the message will depend on my receiving more love for the Lord Jesus and for others. Working this Step consists in both speaking to others and speaking to God about others.

As I surrender my life to God's everlasting love, His love in me may bring wanderers back to Him and give them healing.

PRAYER FOR TODAY

O God, keep me in everlasting fellowship with you throughout eternity. Enable me to help others find fellowship with you and life everlasting.

INDEX

ABOUT THE AUTHORS

Andrew Murray has been recognized as a world master of prayer. His many devotional books have been translated into numerous foreign languages. For over a hundred years, his proven prayer principles have changed thousands of lives. His writings have taught people how to know God, and how to maintain a daily contact with God for direction and power for living— one day at a time. Murray, who pioneered the teaching of abiding in God daily for strength to overcome the challenges of each day, was born in 1828 and died in 1917. During his lifetime he was a noted motivational speaker and world traveler.

L. G. Parkhurst, Jr., has been helping members of Alcoholics Anonymous and Al-Anon complete their Fifth Steps since 1975. To protect the anonymity of alcoholics and other drug users, their families, and friends, he helped start the first Al-Anon group to meet outside of the AA building in Rochester, Minnesota. He has compiled numerous devotional and prayer book classics, including *The Believer's Secret of the Abiding Presence,* from the writings of Andrew

Murray and Brother Lawrence, and *The Believer's Secret of Intercession* from the writings of Andrew Murray and C.H. Spurgeon. In his first book for CompCare Publishers, he combines his knowledge of Andrew Murray's prayer principles with the concerns of those practicing a Twelve Step recovery Program.

More books to enrich your life from CompCare® Publishers!

Parents Who Care Too Much by James M. Farris, Ph.D. Foreword by Jack Felton, coauthor of *Toxic Faith*. A must-read book for parents whose addictive/dysfunctional child is hurling the family toward self-destruction. Family psychologist James M. Farris shows the way out of devastating codependency and into the healing power of love. **#275-3, $11.95**

Surviving the Prodigal Years by Marcia Mitchell. *Surviving the Prodigal Years* provides encouragement, spiritual guidance and hope for surviving the stress-filled and often perplexing teen and young adult years. Marcia Mitchell assures her readers that although they may not be able to change the actions or attitudes of their children, they can find inner peace and strength from God to sustain them through the trials and tribulations of adolescence and young adulthood. **#284-2, $11.00**

A Day at a Time. If you are in recovery or practice daily meditation, join the more than 1 million faithful readers who have discovered these hopeful day-by-day messages. This long-time favorite among Twelve Step group members, with reflections and prayers, will bring comfort and, above all, hope. It is available in four formats: ***Hardcover, #000-9, $6.95, Deluxe, hardcover, #001-7, $10.95, Pocket-size paperback #196-X, $6.95, Audio cassette #126-9, $9.95***

StepTrouble by William L. Coleman. Drawing on his own experiences and on interviews with various stepteens, William Coleman offers insight and advice on setting boundaries in a new stepfamily and dealing with the inevitable frustrations and uncertainties. The perfect gift for any teen about to embark on a journey into the uncharted territory of a new stepfamily. **#284-2, $11.00**

To order, call 1-800-328-3330 and remember to ask for your *FREE* catalog!